PRINCETON UNIVERSITY STUDIES IN PAPYROLOGY

No. 1. Papyri in the Princeton University Collections, Vol. II. Edited with notes by EDMUND HARRIS KASE, JR.

No. 2. Taxation in Egypt from Augustus to Diocletian. By SHERMAN LEROY WALLACE.

No. 3. The John H. Scheide Biblical Papyri: Ezekiel. Edited by ALLAN CHESTER JOHNSON, HENRY SNYDER GEHMAN, and EDMUND HARRIS KASE, JR.

No. 4. Papyri in the Princeton University Collections, Vol. III. Edited with notes by ALLAN CHESTER JOHNSON and SIDNEY PULLMAN GOODRICH.

PAPYRI IN THE PRINCETON UNIVERSITY COLLECTIONS

VOL. III

EDITED WITH NOTES

BY

ALLAN CHESTER JOHNSON

AND

SIDNEY PULLMAN GOODRICH

PRINCETON

PRINCETON UNIVERSITY PRESS

LONDON: HUMPHREY MILFORD, OXFORD UNIVERSITY PRESS

1942

PREFACE

The collections of papyri in the Princeton University Library were acquired through the generosity of Mr. Robert Garrett and Mr. John H. Scheide. With the present volume the work of editing these collections is completed.

Acknowledgments are due to graduate students in the Department of Classics who have assisted in reading and editing these documents. In the present volume Mr. Herbert Long recognized No. 112 as from Xenophon, and Mr. Bruce Metzger edited Nos. 113 and 159. Professors Kase and Youtie have given their assistance freely. The junior editor has borne most of the burden of deciphering the fragments and he has also read the proof and prepared the indices. The funds for publication were provided by the Andrew Fleming West Foundation and by the University Research Fund.

A. C. J.
S. P. G.

TABLE OF CONTENTS

TABLE OF PAPYRI

SIGLA

———

( ) — resolution of abbreviation or symbol.

[ ] — lacuna in original text.

⟦ ⟧ — deletion by editor.

{ } — deletion by scribe or corrector.

⟨ ⟩ — restoration of words omitted by scribe.

` ´ — corrections or additions by scribe above the line.

CLASSICAL TEXTS

108. Iliad I, 209-239

GD 7740   7.0 × 32.0 cm.   2nd century

This fragment comes from a roll as the *verso* is blank. Since top
and bottom are preserved, the column had 31 lines and this fragment
presumably belonged to the eighth column, assuming that Col. I had
22 lines with heading and title. The first book of the Iliad would thus
require 20 columns. We may estimate the width of each column at
about 21 cm., and if the space between each column averaged 6 cm. it
would require almost 5 m. for the complete roll.

Except for the itacism (l. 233) and an evident error in copying
(l. 234) this fragment offers no variants from the standard texts. See
Collart, Revue de Philologie 58(1932), 315-349; 59(1933), 33-61;
63(1939), 289-307, for list of Homeric papyri found since the publication of T. W. Allen's edition.

ἄμφω ὁμ]ῶς θυμῷ φιλ[έουσά τε κηδομένη τε
210 ἀλλ' ἄγε λῆγ'] ἔριδος μηδὲ ξ[ίφος ἕλκεο χειρί·
ἀλλ' ἤτοι ἔ]πεσιν μὲν ὀνε[ίδισον ὡς ἔσεταί περ·
ὧδε γὰρ ἐξ]ερέω, τὸ δὲ καὶ [τετελεσμένον ἔσται·
καί ποτέ τοι] τρὶς τόσσα παρ[έσσεται ἀγλαὰ δῶρα
ὕβριος εἵν]εκα τῆσδε· σὺ [δ' ἴσχεο, πείθεο δ' ἡμῖν.
215 τὴν δ' ἀπα]μειβόμενος π[ροσέφη πόδας ὠκὺς Ἀχιλλεύς·
χρὴ μὲν σφω]ϊτερόν γε, θεά, [ἔπος εἰρύσσασθαι
καὶ μάλα περ] θυμῷ κεχολω[μένον· ὡς γὰρ ἄμεινον
ὅς κε θεοῖς ἐ]πιπείθηται, μ[άλα τ' ἔκλυον αὐτοῦ.
ἦ καὶ ἐπ' ἀργυρ]έῃ κώπῃ σχέ[θε χεῖρα βαρεῖαν
220 ἂψ δ' εἰς κουλε]ὸν ὦσε μέγα [ξίφος, οὐδ' ἀπίθησε
μύθῳ Ἀθηναί]ης ἡ δ' Οὔλυμπ[όνδε βεβήκει
δώματ' ἐς αἰ]γιόχοιο Διὸς με[τὰ δαίμονας ἄλλους.
Πηλεΐδης δ' ἐ]ξαῦτις ἀταρτηρ[οῖς ἐπέεσσιν
Ἀτρείδην προ]σέειπε καὶ οὔ πω [λῆγε χόλοιο·

1

225 οἰνοβα]ρές, κυνὸς ὄμματ᾽ [ἔχων, κραδίην δ᾽ ἐλάφοιο,
    οὔτε πο]τ᾽ ἐς πόλεμον ἅμα λαῷ [θωρηχθῆναι
    οὔτε λό]χονδ᾽ ἰέναι σὺν ἀριστήέ[σσιν ᾿Αχαιῶν
    τέτληκ]ας θυμῷ τα° δέ τοι κὴρ [εἴδεται εἶναι.
    ἦ πολὺ] λώϊόν ἐστι κατὰ στρατ[ὸν εὐρὺν ᾿Αχαιῶν
230 δῶρ᾽ ἀ]ποαιρεῖσθαι ὅστις σέθε[ν ἀντίον εἴπῃ·
    δημ]οβόρος βασιλεύς, ἐπεὶ [οὐτιδανοῖσιν ἀνάσσεις·
    ἦ γὰρ ἄ]ν, ᾿Ατρείδη, νῦν ὕστατα [λωβήσαιο
    ἀλλ᾽ ἔκ] τοι ἐρέω καὶ ἐπεὶ μέγ[αν ὅρκον ὀμοῦμαι
    ναὶ μὰ]τόδε σκῆπρον τὸ μ[ὲν οὔ ποτε φύλλα καὶ ὅζους
235 φύσει, ἐ]πεὶ δὴ πρῶτα τομ[ὴν ἐν ὄρεσσι λέλοιπεν,
    οὐδ᾽ ἀναθηλ]ήσει· περὶ γά[ρ ῥά ἑ χαλκὸς ἔλεψε
    φύλλα τε κα]ὶ φλοιόν· νῦν [αὖτέ μιν υἶες ᾿Αχαιῶν
    ἐν παλάμῃ]ς φορέουσι [δικασπόλοι, οἵ τε θέμιστας
    πρὸς Διὸς εἰρ]ύαται· ὁ δέ τοι [μέγας ἔσσεται ὅρκος·

228. τα corrected to το, apparently by a second hand.
233. επει = επι, the only etacism in this papyrus.
234. σκηπρον = σκηπτρον, an error so natural that it escaped the corrector's notice.

The entire absence of punctuation and diacritical signs (other than the diaeresis) tend to indicate a date not later than the third century; while the absence of *iota adscriptum* combines with the handwriting to place it in the second, or the end of the first century A. D. Cf. Thompson, *Introduction to Greek and Latin palaeography*, 62.

109. ILIAD I. 216-237; 574-597

GD 7656   3.8 × 21 cm.   5th century

This is written in a rather ill-formed uncial hand on a fairly cheap grade of papyrus. The top margin (about 3.3 cm.) is preserved. This leaf evidently formed part of a codex with a rather wide leaf, apparently with four columns of 50-54 lines to a column. A similar length of column is found in the Scheide Biblical papyri. The first leaf of the codex contained Iliad I. 1-215, probably written on the *Recto*, leaving the *Verso* blank or for a title.

There are no departures from the text of Munro and Allen. *Iota adscriptum* is omitted in l. 579 (νεικειησι) but is written elsewhere (ll. 219, 226). No accents, breathings, punctuation, or diaeresis appear in this text.

[χρὴ μὲν σφωΐτερόν γε], θεά, ἔπ[ος εἰρύσασθαι]
[καὶ μάλα περ θυμῷ κ]εχολωμέ[νον· ὡς γὰρ ἄμεινον]
[ὅς κε θεοῖς ἐπιπείθητ]αι, μάλα τ᾽ [ἔκλυον αὐτοῦ,]
[ἦ καὶ ἐπ᾽ ἀργυρέῃ κώ]πῃ σχέθε [χεῖρα βαρεῖαν,]
220 [ἂψ δ᾽ ἐς κουλέον ὦσε] μέγα ξίφ[ος, οὐδ᾽ ἀπίθησε]
[μύθῳ Ἀθηναίης· ἡ] δ᾽ Οὔλυμπό[νδε βεβήκει]
[δώματ᾽ ἐς αἰγιόχοιο Δι]ὸς μετὰ δα[ίμονας ἄλλους,]
[Πηλεΐδης δ᾽ ἐξαῦτις ἀτ]αρτηροῖς [ἐπέεσσιν]
[Ἀτρεΐδην προσέειπε,] καὶ οὔ π[ω λῆγε χόλοιο·]
225 [οἰνοβαρές, κυνὸς ὄμματ᾽ ἔ]χων, κρ[αδίην δ᾽ ἐλάφοιο,]
[οὔτε ποτ᾽ ἐς πόλεμον ἅ]μα λαῷ [θωρηχθῆναι]
[οὔτε λόχονδ᾽ ἰέναι σὺ]ν ἀριστή[εσσιν Ἀχαιῶν]
[τέτληκας θυμῷ· τὸ δέ τοι] κῆρ εἴδε[ται εἶναι.]
[ἦ πολὺ λώϊόν ἐστι] κατὰ στρ[ατὸν εὐρὺν Ἀχαιῶν]
230 [δῶρ᾽ ἀποαιρεῖσθαι ὅς τι]ς σέθεν [ἀντίον εἴπῃ·]
[δημοβόρος βασιλεύ]ς, ἐπεὶ οὐτιδ[ανοῖσιν ἀνάσσεις·]
[ἦ γὰρ ἄν, Ἀτρεΐδη, νῦ]ν ὕστατα λ[ωβήσαιο.]
[ἀλλ᾽ ἔκ τοι ἐρέω κα]ὶ ἐπὶ μέγ[αν ὅρκον ὀμοῦμαι·]
[ναὶ μὰ τόδε σκῆπτρ]ον, τὸ μὲν [οὔ ποτε φύλλα καὶ ὄζους]
235 [φύσει, ἐπεὶ δὴ πρῶτ]α τομὴν ἐ[ν ὄρεσσι λέλοιπεν,]
[οὐδ᾽ ἀναθηλήσει· π]ερὶ γὰρ ῥά ἑ χ[αλκὸς ἔλεψε]
[φύλλα τε καὶ φλοιόν]· νῦν αὐτέ [μιν υἷες Ἀχαιῶν]

[εἰ] δὴ σφὼ ἕνε[κα θνητῶν ἐριδαίνετον ὧδε,]
575 [ἐ]ν δὲ θεοῖσι κολ[ῳὸν ἐλαύνετον· οὐδέ τι δαιτὸς]
[ἐ]σθλῆς ἔσσε[ται ἦδος, ἐπεὶ τὰ χερείονα νικᾷ.]
[μ]ητρὶ δ᾽ ἐγὼ [παράφημι καὶ αὐτῇ περ νοεούσῃ,]
πατρὶ φίλω[ι ἐπὶ ἦρα φέρειν Διί, ὄφρα μὴ αὖτε]
νεικείῃσ[ι πατήρ, σὺν δ᾽ ἡμῖν δαῖτα ταράξῃ.]
580 εἴ περ γάρ κ᾽ [ἐθέλῃσιν Ὀλύμπιος ἀστεροπητὴς]
ἐξ ἑδέων [στυφελίξαι· ὁ γὰρ πολὺ φέρτατός ἐστιν·]
ἀλλὰ σὺ τ[όν γ᾽ ἐπέεσσι καθάπτεσθαι μαλακοῖσιν·]
αὐτίκ᾽ ἔπ[ειθ᾽ ἵλαος Ὀλύμπιος ἔσσεται ἡμῖν.]
ὣς ἄρ᾽ ἔφη, [καὶ ἀναΐξας δέπας ἀμφικύπελλον]
585 μητρὶ φίλ[ῃ ἐν χειρὶ τίθει, καί μιν προσέειπε·]

τέτλαθι, [μῆτερ ἐμή, καὶ ἀνάσχεο κηδομένη περ,]
μή σε φ[ί]λ[ην περ ἐοῦσαν ἐν ὀφθαλμοῖσιν ἴδωμαι]
θεινομ[ένην, τότε δ' οὔ τι δυνήσομαι ἀχνύμενός περ]
χραισμ[εῖν· ἀργαλέος γὰρ 'Ολύμπιος ἀντιφέρεσθαι·]
590 ἤδη γάρ [με καὶ ἄλλοτ' ἀλεξέμεναι μεμαῶτα]
ῥῖψε πο[δὸς τεταγὼν ἀπὸ βηλοῦ θεσπεσίοιο,]
πᾶν δ' [ἦμαρ φερόμην, ἅμα δ' ἠελίῳ καταδύντι]
κάππε[σον ἐν Λήμνῳ, ὀλίγος δ' ἔτι θυμὸς ἐνῆεν·]
ἔνθά μ[ε Σίντιες ἄνδρες ἄφαρ κομίσαντο πεσόντα.]
595 ὣς φάτ[ο, μείδησεν δὲ θεὰ λευκώλενος Ἥρη,]
μειδήσ[ασα δὲ παιδὸς ἐδέξατο χειρὶ κύπελλον·]
αὐτὰρ [ὁ τοῖς ἄλλοισι θεοῖς ἐνδέξια πᾶσιν]

110. ILIAD IV. 378-384

AM 11227 E   3.2 × 4.5 cm.   1st or 2nd century

Written in a large, handsome uncial, this tiny fragment is apparently
from a roll, as the *verso* is blank. It presents no variants from the
Oxford Text of Monro and Allen.

οἱ δὲ τότ' ἐστρατόωνθ' ἱερὰ] πρὸς τείχε[α Θήβης
καί ρα μάλα λίσσοντο δόμ]εν κλειτο[ὺς ἐπικούρους
380 οἱ δ' ἔθελον δόμεναι καὶ ἐπ]ήνεον ὡς [ἐκέλευον
ἀλλὰ Ζεὺς ἔτρεψε παραίσια σ]ήματα φα[ίνων
οἱ δ' ἐπεὶ οὖν ᾤχοντο ἰδὲ πρὸ]όδοῦ ἐγέν[οντο
'Ασωπὸν δ' ἵκοντα βαθύσχοι]νον λεχεπ[οίην
ἔνθ' αὖτ' ἀγγελίην ἐπὶ Τυδῆ σ]τεῖλαν 'Αχα[ιοί.

111. ILIAD VI. 1-15; 25-39

GD 7533   9.8 × 8.5 cm.   3rd century

Fragment from the upper inner portion of a codex leaf containing
the beginning of Iliad VI. The *recto* contains lines 1-15 and the heading, the *verso* contains lines 25-39. There were originally, it seems,
about 24 lines to the page. The hand is a fairly small uncial of the third

century, resembling that of the Mimes of Herodas in general style, but not in detail. The diaeresis is consistently used, and the apostrophe appears once (line 8); but no other diacritical marks are used. *Iota adscriptum* is omitted in l. 7 Θρηκ[εσ]σι, l. 10 μετώπῳ, and l. 39 [μυρ]ικίνῳ, but otherwise it is consistently and correctly used.

The text presents no variations from that of Monro and Allen (Oxford Classical Texts).

Ἰ[λιάδος Ζ]

Τρώων δ' οἰώθη καὶ Ἀχαι[ῶν] φ[ύλοπις] αἰνή
πολλὰ δ' ἄρ' ἔνθα καὶ ἔνθ' ἴθ[υσε μάχη πεδίοιο]
ἀλλήλων ἰθυνομένων χ[αλκήρεα δοῦρα]
μεσσηγὺς Σιμόεντος ἰδὲ Ξάνθοι[ο ῥοάων]
5 Αἴας δὲ πρῶτος Τελαμώνιος ἔρ[κος Ἀχαίων]
Τρώων ῥῆξε φάλαγγα φόως δ' ἑ[τάροισ]ιν [ἔθηκεν]
ἄνδρα βαλὼν ὃς ἄριστος ἐνὶ Θρήκ[εσ]σι τέτ[υκτο]
υ[ἱ]ὸν Ἐϋσσώρ[ο]υ Ἀκάμαντ' ἠΰν τ[ε] μέ[γαν τε]
τὸν ῥ' ἔβαλε πρῶτος κόρυθος φάλ[ον ἱπποδασείης]
10 ἐν δὲ μετώπῳ πῆξε, πέρησε δ' ἄρ' [ὀστέον εἴσω]
α[ἰ]χμὴ χαλκείη τὸν δὲ σκότος ὄσσε [κάλυψεν]
Ἄξυλον δ' ἄρ' ἔπεφνε βοὴν ἀγαθὸς Δ[ιομήδης]
Τευθρανίδ[η]ν ὃς ἔναιεν ἐΰκτιμ[ένη ἐν Ἀρίσβῃ]
[ἀ]φν[ει]ὸς [βιότο]ι[ο φ]ίλος δ' ἦν ἀν[θρώποισι]
15 [πά]ντας γὰρ φιλέεσκ[εν] ὁδῶι [ἔπι οἰκία ναίων]

25 [ποιμαίνω]ν δ' ἐπ' ὄε[σσ]ι [μίγη] φι[λό]τητι καὶ εὐνῆι
[ἡ δ' ὑποκυσαμένη διδυμ]άονε γείνα[τ]ο παῖδε,
[καὶ μὲν τῶν ὑπέλυσε μ]ένος κα[ὶ] φαίδιμα γυῖα
[Μηκιστηϊάδης καὶ] ἀπ' ὤμ[ω]ν τεύχε' ἔσυλα
[Ἀστύαλον δ' ἄρ' ἔπεφ]νε μενεπτόλεμος Πολυποίτης
30 [Πιδύτην δ' Ὀ]δυσ[εὺς] Περκώσιον ἐξενάριξεν
[ἔγχεϊ χαλκεί]ωι Τε[ῦκρ]ος δ' Ἀρε[τ]άον[α δῖο]ν
[Ἀντίλοχος δ' Ἄ]βλη[ρον] ἐνήρα[το] δ[ο]υρὶ φαεινῶι
[Νεστορίδης, Ἔλατο]ν [δ]ὲ ἄρα[ξ ἀνδρῶ]ν Ἀγαμ[έμ]νων
[ναῖε δὲ Σατνιόεντος ἐ]ϋρ[ρείταο παρ'] ὄχ[θας]
35 [Πήδασον αἰπειν]ήν, Φύλακ[ον δ'] ἕλ[ε Λήϊτος ἥ]ρ[ως]

[φεύγοντ' Εὐρύπυ]λος δὲ Μελάνθιον [ἐξεν]άριξ[ε]ν.
["Αδρηστον δ' ἄρ' ἔπ]ειτα β[ο]ὴ[ν] ἀγαθὸς Μενέλαος
[ζωὸν ἔλ' ἵππω γάρ οἱ ἀ]τυζομένω πεδίοιο
[ὄζῳ ἔνι βλαφθέντε μυρ]ικίνῳ, ἀ[γ]κύ[λο]ν ἅρμ[α]

112. XENOPHON, HELLENICA

AM 11243   4th century

Three small pieces of parchment (Frag. I, 4 × 5.5 cm.; II, 3.5 ×
6 cm.; III, 4 × 4 cm.) had been glued together by the finder, probably
to make a more impressive showing to a possible buyer. The parchment
is very thin and fragile. Every second line was ruled, and the writing
is in minute uncials of the style of the fourth century. The original was
evidently a folio with each leaf having two columns which averaged 19
letters to a line and 32 lines in each column. Fragments I and II
belong to the same folio, and if No. I is placed near the top of the first
column, II belongs about half way down the second column.

The text offers little variation from the MSS of the Hellenica except
such errors as are due to carelessness on the part of the scribe.

I *recto*. Hellenica I. 6. 30.

[τὸ δὲ δεξιὸ]ν [κ]έρας
[Πρωτόμαχος εἶχε] πέντε
[καὶ δέκα ναῦς] παρὰ δ' αὐτὸν
[Θρασύλλος] ἑτέραις πέντε
5 [καὶ δέκα να]ῦς ἐπετέτακτο
[δὲ Πρωτομάχῳ μὲν Λ]υσίας ἔ-
[χων τὰς ἴσας ναῦς] Θρασύλ-
[λῳ δὲ 'Αριστογένη]ς οὕτω
[δὲ ἐτάχθησαν ἵνα μὴ] δι-
10 έκπλουν διδοῖεν κτλ.

3. ναῦς 1. ναυσί   4. ἑτέρας 1. ἑτέραις

II *recto*. Hellenica I. 6. 34.

[   ]ἀπώλον-
[το δὲ τῶν μὲν ᾿Α]θηναίων
[νῆες πέντε καὶ] εἴκοσιν
[αὐτοῖς ἀνδράσιν] ἐκτὸς
5 [ὀλίγων τῶν πρὸς] τὴν γῆν
[προσενεχθέντων] τῶν δὲ Πε-
[λοποννησίων Λ]ακωνι-
[καὶ μὲν ἐννέα πασῶν] οὐσῶν
[δέκα, τῶν δ᾽ ἄλλων σ]υμ[μ]ά-
10 [χων πλείους ἢ ἑξή]κον-
[τα. ἔδοξε δὲ τοῖς τῶν ᾿Αθ]ηναίων
[στρατηγοῖς ἑπτὰ μὲ]ν καὶ [τετταρά-
κοντα κτλ.

II *verso*. Hellenica I. 6. 36-7.

    [δια-]
λέγεσθαι, παρ[αχρῆμα δὲ αὖθις]
πλεῖν εἰς τὸ [ἑαυτῶν στρα-]
τόπεδον ἐ[στεφανωμέ-]
5 νους κα[ὶ βοῶντας ὅτι Καλ-]
λικρατίδα[ς νενίκηκε ναυ-]
μαχῶν κα[ὶ ὅτι αἱ τῶν ᾿Αθη-]
ναίων νῆ[ες ἀπολώλασιν]
[ἅ]πασαι [καὶ οἱ μὲν τοῦτ᾽]
10 [ἐ]ποίο[υν αὐτὸς δ᾽ ἐπειδὴ]
ἐκε[ῖνοι κατέπλεον ἔθυε τὰ]
[εὐαγγέλια καὶ τοῖς στρα-]
τι[ώταις κτλ.   ]

I *verso*. Hellenica I. 6. 38.

    ἐπεὶ οἵ
τε[πολέμιοι ἀπεδεδράκε-]
σαν καὶ ὁ ἄνεμ[ος εὐδιαί-]
τερος ἦν, ἀπαν[τήσας τοῖς]
5 ᾿Αθηναίοις ἤδ[η ἀνηγμέ-]

νοις ἐκ τῶν Ἀρ[γινουσῶν]
ἔφρασε [τὰ περὶ τοῦ Ἐτεο-]
νίκου [οἱ δὲ Ἀθηναῖοι κα-]
τέπλευσ[αν εἰς τὴν Μυτι-]
10 λήνην, κτλ.]

III *recto.* Hellenica I. 7. 30.

ἕκα[στον]
[ἐκ τῆς αὐτοῦ συμμ]οιρας
[τῶν στρατη]γῶν ὀκτὼ ὄν-
[των καὶ τὰ]ς τῶν ταξιάρχων
· 5 [δέκα καὶ τὰς] Σαμίων δέκα
[καὶ τὰς τῶν ναυ]άρχων τρεῖς
[αὗται ἅπασαι γίγνο]νται ἑπτὰ
[καὶ τετταράκοντα τέτταρες
κτλ]

2. συμμοιρας 1. συμμορίας

III *verso.* Hellenica I. 7. 32.

μάρ[τυρες οἱ σωθέντες ἀ-]
πὸ τ[οῦ αὐτομάτου ὧν]
ἦν τῶν στρ[ατηγῶν ἐπὶ κα-]
ταδύσης νεὼς [διασωθεὶς ὂν]
5 κελεύουσι [τῇ αὐτῇ ψήφῳ]
κ[ρ]ίνε[σθαι καὶ αὐτὸν τότε]
δε[όμ]ενον [ἀναιρέσεως κτλ.

3. ἦν 1. εἰς

113. ISOCRATES, ANTIDOSIS, 16-18

GD 7527   7.5 × 9.5 cm.   2nd century

This fragment is part of a roll on which the text was written in neat
uncials in columns averaging twelve letters to the line. The number
of lines to the column cannot be determined, but the insertion of the
omitted passage from sec. 18 must be made immediately after the 26th
line, and probably there were at least 30 lines in the column.

The correction at the top of the column is written by a second hand. The *coronis* at the left was probably duplicated at line 26 to indicate where the passage was to be inserted. Furthermore the word κάτ(ω) at the end of the passage served to remind the reader to look below.

The only variant from the standard MSS is οὐδέν for μηδέν in l. 2. In l. 8 a colon was inserted by the first hand. The following *phi* was marked by a dot above it as a sign of omission, but a slanting stroke was drawn through by a corrector using different ink, who also added the diaeresis over the following *iota*, and indicated the elision by an apostrophe over the *nu*.

For literary texts of Isocrates, see Oldfather, The Greek Literary Texts from Graeco-Roman Egypt (University of Wisconsin Studies in the Social Sciences and History, No. 9, 1923). Since that time a few other fragments of Isocrates have been listed in Aegyptus, but none of these come from the Antidosis.

(Hand 2)　　ἐνθυμουμένους ὅτι
　　　　　　οὐδὲν ἔδει δίδοσθαι
　　ς'　　　τοῖς φεύγουσιν ,　　　　κάτ(ω)
(Hand 1)　　λας ἐμοῦ δὲ Λυσί-
　　　　　　μαχος αὐτοὺς
　　　　　　τοὺς λόγους μά-
　　　　　　λιστα διαβέβλη-
　　5　　κεν · {φ} ἵν' ἦν μὲν
　　　　　　ἰ[κα]νῶς δόξ[ω]λέ-
　　　　　　γειν ἔνοχος ὢν
　　　　　　φανῶ τοῖς ὑπ[ὸ]

2. οὐδέν is better grammatically, but in view of Isocrates' fondness for avoiding hiatus, μηδέν has gained acceptance though its construction with the following infinitive is awkward.

114. MEDICAL TREATISE

GD 7601　　　　　　8.0 × 20.5 cm.　　　　　2nd or 3rd century

The papyrus presents parts of two columns, written in the colorless uncials of the second or third century. The letters average 3 or 4 mm. in height. There are 25 lines to a column, so that the column measures

14.2 cm. in height, leaving approximately equal margins of 3.1 cm. at top and bottom. The space between the columns averages about 2 cm., but the remains of col. I show that the lines were very uneven in length. The width of a column cannot be determined, although it seems likely that more than half of col. II is preserved.

The text apparently deals with the treatment of some illness (the common cold?). Although there are echos of Hippocratic theory ($\pi\nu\epsilon\dot{\nu}\mu\alpha\tau$ος $\kappa\iota\nu\dot{\eta}\sigma\epsilon\omega$ς and the reiteration of $\theta\epsilon\rho\mu\dot{o}$ς and its derivatives), these do not indicate Hippocratic origin, for they had become part of the medical cant of antiquity. The emphasis on treatment and the practical tone of the text generally suggest rather the Empiric or Methodist school.

The treatment is quite similar to that recommended by Celsus for *gravedines* (colds) :

IV. 5. 3-4:

Ubi aliquid eiusmodi sensimus, protinus abstinere a sole [cf. 1. 42], balneo, vino, venere debemus; inter quae unctione [cf. 1. 41] adsueto cibo nihilo minus uti licet. Ambulatione tantum acri sed tecta utendum est [cf. 1. 50]; post eam caput atque os supra quinquagiens perfricandum. Raroque fit ut, si biduo vel certe triduo nobis temperavimus id vitium non levetur. Quo levato, *si* in destillatione crassa facta pituita est, vel in gravedine nares magis patent, balneo utendum est [cf. 1. 37?], multaque aqua prius calida, post egelida fovendum os caputque; deinde cum cibo pleniore [cf. 1. 45] vinum bibendum.

IV. 5. 6:

protinus primis diebus multum ambulandum [cf. 1. 50, 31?] est; perfricandae vehementer inferiores partes, etc. usque ad finem capitis IV. 5.

The papyri of medical content published since 1931 are:

        P Aberdeen 8-11, 123-5
        P Giss 45
        P Lund 6 (pharmacy)
        P Lund 7 (anatomy)
        P Mil 14 (nerves)
        P Mil 15
        P Mil 16 (pharmacy)
        P Oslo 72
        PSI 1180
        P Str lit. 8 (Etudes de papyrologie 3 [1936] p. 90)
        P Wien xxxii
        Studi Italiani di Filologia classica, N.S. 12 (1935) 93-94

Col. I

]. ν προ
]
]
]
5]ϝες ἀπὸ
]λοτον
]ωματι
]μα
]σιν τας
10]ωστει
]νεπου
].μεις
]ν καὶ
]ων
15]διαθερ
]καὶ
]γοις
].ας πο
].α α
20]ιον
].οις
]ν συ
]και
]ν υ
25]πνευ-

Col. II

ματος κεινήσεω[ς
ἐν τῶ ὄκνω θερμα[
γειν[ο]μένου ἀνὰ π[
σεσθαι καὶ ἀραιῶσθ[αι
30 τα ἐξ ἐπιστολῆς τρ[
ον δὲ προβαίνοντ[α
οἷοις ἀναγκαῖόν ἐσ[τι
βάθους τινῶν ἀπει[
διαφορεῖσαι διὰ [τ]ῶ[ν
35 σεως καὶ [μ]άλιστα ῳ[
ρατον τοὺ[ς] ἐπινομ[
νει ἀποξηραίνεσθαι [
ρον καὶ ἑλκώδη τὸν [τὴν]
θεραπείαν μὲν οὖν [ἀ-]
40 ναγκαιοτάτην εἶναι [ἄλει-]
ψιν ἐν πολλῶ ἐλαίω [
ρον μηδὲ ἐν θερμῶ [
θερμότερον καὶ πω[ὑ-]
περβαίνειν ὅπως μὴ [
45 ται καὶ τὴν τροφὴν [ἀ-]
ποστέλλοντα τῶν ξ[
ὑγροῦ τὴν δόσιν κατα[
σθω διὰ τοῦ ῥινὸς καὶ .[
νεσθαι κα[τὰ] τὸν ἐν κα[
50 ωρα γυμνάζωνται ..[

115. PHILOSOPHICAL TREATISE(?)

AM 11227 C   5.0 × 5.2 cm.   2nd or 3rd century

Traces of erasures on the *recto* indicate that this fragment is a palimpsest.

Recto

]τοῖς φιλομαθοῦσι τω[
]τὴν χρησιμὴν ὑπὲρ[
]ος χρᾶσθαι καὶ μὴ λ[
π]ροκειμένην ἀναπ[
]πημάτων ὅπως[
].....[

Verso

]κείνης ἀπὸ γεω[
τ]ῶν ἡμερῶν ἢ ὀπ[
]ἑλκεις τὰ ὑπομ[νήματα
]μου οιῆ`ο' ....[

OFFICIAL DOCUMENTS

A. PETITIONS

116. Petition

GD 7534   9.4 × 13.1 cm.   1st century B. C.

This document is written in large clear uncials. The papyrus is badly worm-eaten and has been patched on the verso. It was folded in narrow strips, and it is not quite clear whether one or two folds may not have been lost after line 3.

The petitions of the Ptolemaic period are to be found in the collection of Gueraud, *Enteuxeis*.

'Αλεξάνδρωι ἀξιῶ σε
ἐ[ὰν] φαίνηται ἐν ὧ
τ[. . . . .]ο [. . . . .]ουν
. . . .
5 [   ]κυρ[. . . . .]
καὶ ἐν ἀρχηι ὑπέσχου
συνελθεῖν τὸν Ζώι-
λον ὁπ . . . . καῖρος
αὐτῶι παραδῶι ἀξι-
10 ώσηι ὑπὲρ τῶν κα-
τ' ἐμὲ συνπαράλαβε
δὲ ὅσους ἂν δυνῆι
ἐπὶ τῆ[ς . .]ση . . ς
εὐτύχει.

117. Petition

GD 7518   12.5 × 22.5 cm.   52 or 3 B. C.

Thaesis, a tenant of a cleruchic allotment, had deposited 293 artabas of wheat with Tesenouphis. When he refused to acknowledge the

12

deposit or return it, she appealed to the strategus. Further proceedings are obscure. Some proposal was made for repayment of the deposit in the 27th year, but Thaesis, who wanted to arrest the man, made some promise to somebody who had a letter written to the toparch. The superintendent of local police was instructed to arrest Tesenouphis. But the latter had never been brought before the strategus. Thaesis now asks that Tesenouphis be brought to trial that she may receive justice. Below the petition is a memorandum which apparently gave the outcome of the trial.

The difficult hand and the mutilated condition of the document do not aid in easy understanding of the content. The 27th year helps to determine the date in the first century before Christ to which period the hand belongs. If in the reign of Ptolemy Auletes the 27th year is 52 B. C.; if in the reign of Augustus the document is to be dated 3 B. C. Calderini (Θησαυροί, p. 41) states that no private storehouses are known from the Ptolemaic period. This may be accidental, but it throws the balance in favor of the later date.

[τ]ῶι στρατη[γῶι   ]
παρὰ Θαήσιος τῆς Χ[......]τῶν ἐκ Φιλαδελφείας
[ἀ]πέδωκά σοι ὑπόμ[νη]μα κατὰ Τεσε-
[ν]ούφιος θησαυροφύλακος τοῦ ᾿Αντι-
5 [φ]ίλου ἰδιωτικοῦ θησ[α]υροῦ προφερο-
[μ]ένη[........] παραθεμέ-
[ν]ην με α[ὐ]τῶι ἐν τ[ῶι θ]ησαυρῶι (ἀρτάβας πυροῦ) σϙγ
[....]σασθ[αι]μ[........ αὐ]τὰς ἐμὲ
συνπεριενεχθῆναι αὐτῶι ἐφ᾿ ὧι
10 ἐν τῶι [(ἔτει)]κζ ἀποδώσειεν {καὶ} βουλο-
μένη αὐ[τ]ὸ[ν συ]νλ[α]βεῖν ὑπεσχόμην καὶ [ἐ]γρ[ά]ψατο ἐπιστολὴν
εἰς τοπάρ[χην .....]την Πτολεμαίου
ρη̅ ὀνόμ[ατι οὗ] καὶ γεωργῶ τὸν κλῆ-
15 ρον. ἔγραψας Σαραπίωνι τῶι ἐπισ-
τάτει. ἔ[πει]τα καὶ ὁμόλογος γενόμενος συνέσχεν αὐτόν. ἐπεὶ οὖν
ἐντυχοῦσ[ά] σοι συνέταξας τῶι
Σ[α]ραπίων[ι] καταστῆσαι αὐτόν.

20 τούτου δὲ μὴ καθεσταμένου
   ἀ[ξι]ῶ σε ἐπὶ τῶν τόπων εἰ
   β[ούληι ὄν]τα μοι ἐπαναγκάσαι
   [Σαραπ]ίωνα καταστῆσαι
   τ[ὸν ἄνθρ]ωπον ὅπως τύχω
25 τ[οῦ δικαίου.]

                    εὐτύχει
(2nd hand)   ]Ἐπεὶφ παραθέσεως ἔγκ[λημα]
             ]τη . . οργηι . εὔξομαι τοὺς γρ . . . .
             ]αὐτῆι δεῖ τὰς λιπ(ούσας) (ἀρτάβας πυροῦ) σϙγ
30]ἐπὶ κζ (ἔτους) γεν . . . . . .

" To the strategus . . . . . . from Thaesis, daughter of . . . ., from Philadelphia. I have already given you a memorial against Tesenouphis guard of the private treasury of Antiphilus stating that . . . . having stored with him 293 artabas of wheat in his store-room and on demanding (?) their return (he claimed) that I was involved in an agreement (?) that he might return the property in the 27th year. Wishing to arrest the man I agreed and he had a letter written to the toparch X son of Ptolemaeus owner of a 100-ar. allotment in whose name I cultivate. You wrote to Sarapion, superintendent of police. He arrested him since he was an acknowledged defaulter in returning the deposit (?). When I appealed to you, you ordered Sarapion to produce him. Since he has not done so, I beg of you if you will when you are on circuit here to compel Sarapion to produce the man that I may receive justice. Farewell."

4. Antiphilus, apparently the owner of a large estate, is otherwise unknown.

6-8. The papyrus is badly broken here and while the upper and lower portions appear to be firmly joined at one point, it is possible that something has been lost or perhaps omitted by the scribe. At the beginning of line 8 it is possible to restore [αἰτή]σασθαι μ[έλλουσαν αὐ]τὰς.

11-12. The meaning is obscure. Apparently Thaesis wished to arrest Tesenouphis, but the usual meaning of ὑπεσχόμην implies a promise or agreement but to whom or with whom is not clear unless it was an arrangement with Tesenouphis himself. If so, the order to arrest him (line 15 ff.) seems inexplicable. Similarly the subject of ἐγράψατο is not clear, possibly the person with whom Thaesis made her agreement. If this was Tesenouphis, the letter may have had for its purpose some explanation of the reason for the non-payment of rent or taxes by Thaesis who is apparently cultivating land owned by the toparch.

15. Sarapion is probably ἐπιστάτης φυλακιτῶν. He is not to be identified with the superintendent of police at Euhemeria bearing the same name (P. Lond. 895; P. Ryl. II. p. 118).

16. ὁμόλογος γενόμενος. The construction implies that this phrase refers to Sarapion, If so, it is necessary to assume that Sarapion and Tesenouphis were in collusion in some way. However it seems to make sense to take this phrase as in loose grammatical construction with αὐτόν, and interpret it as indicating the guilt of Tesenouphis in not returning the deposit. On the other hand Sarapion seems to have disobeyed the order of the strategus to produce the defendant when required.

18. The space does not allow any other restoration than ἐντυχοῦσα which seems to be used loosely in an absolute construction. For συνέταξας read συνέταξας.

21. This formula is common in appeals, see Guerand, Enteuxeis, passim.

118. Appeal

AM 11227 A   6 × 15 cm.   2nd century

This fragment seemingly contains an appeal concerning property whose ownership was disputed (cf. P. O. 67, A. D. 337).

```
            ].θ ..................ρ ....
            ].. πολλάκις τὰ αὐτὰ διεξιὼν ...
         τ]ῆς σῆς εὐτόνου ἐπεξελεύσεως μ...
         τ]οῦ βιβλειδίου ὅλου ἔτους καὶ η...
    5    ]ω ἐπάρχω Αἰγύπτου π[αρὰ...
         ]εξεῖμεν ἐπ᾽ ἄλλου τὴν ἀξίωσι[ν...
         ]σίου μο[υ] ἀποφάσει παρ[ὰ] πάντω[ν...
         ]ας ἀγαθῇ τύχῃ σε τὸν δικασ[τὴν ...
         ]τὸ διήγημ[α ἐ]π[ὶ] ὅλον τὸ βιβλεί[διον ...
   10    ]γράφων πρὸ[ς τὴν] ἐπίδ[οσιν] κατ[ὰ ...
         ]πρὸς αὐτοῦ δ....ου ἐκδια..κι...
         ].α καταλέλειπ[τα]ί τινα ὑπ....
         ]οἱ ἐκείνης υἱοὶ καὶ κληρονόμοι ...
         ]έδοξαν ἀποφάσεως τῇ[ς ..]σα......
   15    ]α ἅπαξ δὲ ἐρισθέντες παραλ.....
      ἡγε]μονεύσαντι καὶ αὐτῶ κατὰ μου ...
         ]οὐδενὸς παρόντος οὐδὲ ἀντιλέγοντος...
   Σεμπ(?)]ρονίας Σεουηρείνου δὲ ἐπιδεδ[ωκ....
         ]σίου τὸ πρᾶγμα μένειν ἕως ἂν ....
   20    ].ωσφιος νομίμως ἐγένετο μ....
         ]εἰς τοὺς .ις καὶ δεύτερον βιβλ[είδιον ...
         ](ἔτους) δ Φαῶφι κθ τῶ ἱστω .∴.
         ].οι πρὸς .....τῶ ἡγεμονεύσα[ντι
         ]ς μὴ λεγομεν... ι τοῦτο ψεύδ[εται
   25    ]ασιν πρω......κλητὸς ἐν ....
         ]σει καὶ ἔτυχε ὑπ[ογ]ραφῆς τῆς δ.....
         ]ονίας η......κλητὸς μὴ ἐπλ.....
         ]κατὰ τὰ ...ην..ιν.ν τὴν ὑπ[
```

]ειτων τὸ βιβλείδιον Ἰούλιαν[
30   ]ω αὐτῶ . . .ος Αὐρηλίου Νε[
Ἐ]ρμωνθ[ίτου] νομοῦ διακειμεν[
μητρο]οπόλεως τοῦ Ἑρμωνθίτου [ν]ομο[ῦ]

119. PETITION

GD 7531   64.0 × 25.0 cm.   Early 4th century

In the reign of Diocletian a certain Theon, possibly one of his officers
or soldiers during the Emperor's Egyptian campaign, founded an estate
partly by grant (if that is the meaning of the phrase τὰ ὑπ' ἐκίνων
δοθέντα, 31 f.) and partly by purchase. On his death the property was
divided amongst his children and apparently they or their guardians
are parties to the present suit. Theon had a brother named Dionysius
and it seems a fair assumption that this is the ex-protector, a member
of the imperial body-guard, mentioned in line 1. There was also a son
Sarapion apparently a minor at the death of Theon but whether he is
the adjutant (βοηθός) in line 8 or still a minor is nowhere made clear.
It is a fair assumption that uncle Dionysius was acting as guardian if
there were minors in the family. It is also probable that Ammonius,
the beneficiarius, was a son of Theon or a near relative acting as
guardian. Suit against the heirs had been brought by a certain Dioscorus. Apparently he had dropped out of the case shortly before this
memorandum had been drawn up, and his son Macrobius was now the
active prosecutor.

The document is written in a florid style which helps to conceal the
issue. Theon had brought under cultivation waste land and among
other things had planted a vineyard. The heirs claimed that this had
been surveyed and was subject to tax. Even if there might be a slight
carelessness in registration the military tax had been paid. On the
other hand Dioscorus claimed that the estate had never paid taxes and
demanded that the property be surrendered to himself as a reward for
delation. The heirs of Theon deny that the laws allow any such reward
and ask that Dioscorus be impeached for *calumnia*. They now proceed
to rebut the plea of Dioscorus that they have acknowledged the lack of
declaration. To this the heirs reply that it was Dioscorus who made

this statement. The land has been surveyed and the taxes paid. To be sure the surveyor might find the survey did not always agree with the declaration, but that was to be expected, and in such cases they did not, as was the regular practice in the province, make objections to his report but paid the full amount. After expressing some pious platitudes about libellous actions and the hatred of the rulers towards informers, they ask that the suit be voided.

Under Diocletian the survey and declaration of land was attended with strict formalities. The owner of the property took an oath by the Fortune and Victory of the Emperors. The survey was attested by two surveyors, three *juratores*, the adjutant of the decaproti, and the horiodictes (Boak, Etudes de Papyrologie III 26 ff.). Although all declarations could hardly have been checked in this way, it is probable that the new system of taxation inaugurated by Diocletian called for a careful survey. These declarations were filed and the taxes which were paid were not only recorded but receipts were issued. The defendants offer none of these things in evidence, and this leads to the suspicion that their case was weak. Probably Theon had relied on his position as one of Diocletian's staff to evade a proper survey of his grant and his heirs apparently relied on their wealth and influence to escape the present action.

The only clue to provenience is the cleruchy of Nicanor. At Oxyrhynchus Nicanor and Drimacus had a joint allotment (P. O. 250, 1687) and one was assigned to Nicanor Thessalus (P. O. 1534). At Tebtynis Nicanor had an allotment of 100 ar. (P. Teb. 118, 815, etc.).

ψ(ευδο)λογείᾳ ὑπ(ὲρ) Διονυσίου ἀπὸ προτηκόρων καὶ
            Ἀμμωνίου β(ενε)φ(ικιαρίου)
Ἀ(ντίδικος) Διόσκορος ἤτοι ὁ τούτου παῖς Μακρόβιος
τοὺς περιεργαζομένους τὰς ἀλλοτρίας κτήσεις καὶ ἔνδιξιν
[ἐ]πιχιροῦντας μισοῦσιν μὲν οἱ νόμοι μισεῖ δὲ καὶ ἡ σὴ μισο-
5 πονηρία. τοῦτο τοίνυν ἐπιδιχθήσεται πεποιηκὼς ‖ καὶ ‖
Διόσκορος καὶ τιμωρίας ἄξιος, ὡς ἐκ τῶν μελλόντων
ῥηθήσ[ε]σθαι καταφανὲς ἔσται. Θέων ὁ πατὴρ μὲν τοῦ
βοηθ(οῦ) ἀδελφὸς δὲ Διονυσίου ἔτι περιὼν γῆν ἀπεγράψατο
ἐπὶ τοῦ ἐν θεοῖς Διοκλητιάνου ἐν κλήρῳ Νικάνορος,
10 ἐώνηται δὲ καὶ ἑτέραν· καὶ φίλεργος ὢν πολλὰ κατανή-

λωσεν καὶ ἐν ἀμπέλῳ τι μέρος καταφύτευσεν, ἑτέραν
δὲ γῆν καὶ σιτοφόρον ἡμέρωσεν καὶ ἐγεώργι καὶ τὴν
νομὴν εἶχεν. χρόνος πολὺς διελήλυθεν ἐξ ἐκίνου
ἄχρι το[ῦ] παρόντος. νεμηθέντων καὶ τῶν παιδῶν με-
15 τὰ τὴν το[ῦ π]ατρὸς τελευτήν, ἀλλὰ Σαραπίωνος τότε
πρὸς τ[ῇ ἀφ]ηλικότητι ὄντος καὶ τῆς νέας ἀμπέλου
ἀναμε[ρισμέν]ης ἔτι καὶ τοῦ πατρὸς Θέωνος περιόντος,
συμβέβη[κεν] καὶ ταύτην τὴν ἀνακτηθεῖσαν ἐν
ἀμπέλῳ μέτροις ὑποβληθῆναι καὶ ὑποτελῆ γενέσθαι,
20 προσγραφῆναι τοῖς βοηθ(οῖς) ἀμέλι, καὶ ὑπὲρ ταύτης εἰσ-
φέρουσιν τὰς εὐθενίας τὰς στρατιωτικὰς τῷ
ἱερωτάτῳ ταμείῳ ἀλλὰ Διόσκορος ἤτοι ὁ τούτου παῖς
ἐπ᾿ ὀνόματος τοῦ πατρός, ὡς ἀρτίως ἔγνωμεν,
          πρ⟨ὸ⟩ς
ἀναφέρι   τὴν σὴν εὐσέβιαν ἄντικρυς δηλατορίαν
25 τολμῶν, καὶ ὁμολογῖ μὲν καὶ αὐτὸς ἐξ ἀρχαῖς ὑφ᾿
ἡμῶν τὰ γῄδια καὶ γεωργῖσθαι καὶ ἐν ἀμπέλῳ

II   καταπεφυ[τε]ῦσθαι, ψευδόμενος δέ φησιν ἀτελῆ εἶναι καὶ
μηδοτιοῦν παρέχιν τῷ ἱερωτάτῳ ταμείῳ ὁπότε,
ὡς ἔφαμεν, καὶ τὸ ἐν ἀμπέλῳ ὑφ᾿ ἡμῶν καταφυτευ-
30 θὲν ὑπὸ τοῦ ἐκπεμφθέντος κηνσίτορος ὕστερον ἀνε-
μετρήθη καὶ ὑποτελὲς γέγονεν. ἠξίωσέν τε τὰ ὑπ᾿ ἐ-
κίνων δοθέντα καὶ καλλιεργηθέντα αὐτῷ παραδο-
θῆναι, ὁπότε οὐδεὶς νόμος ἐπιτρέπι. ἐπιδὴ τοίνυν
οὐ δῖ τὰς ἀλλοτρίας κτήσεις περιεργάζεσθαι, εἴτε ἐπ᾿
35 ἐλάτ᾿τονι εἴτε ἐπὶ μικρῷ πλέον καθεστήκασιν,
ἀλλ᾿ ἐπιδὴ οἱ νόμοι τοῖς ἐκπονέσασιν προσκυροῦσιν, ἐκῖνος δὲ
περιφανῶ[ς] ὁμολογήσας ὑφ᾿ ἡμῶν ταῦτα κατέχεσθαι
καὶ γεωργῖσθαι ἠθέλησεν δηλατορίαν εἰσαγαγῖν, δεόμεθα
μηδὲν μὲν νεωτερίζεσθαι τὴν δὲ ἐγγραφὴν τὴν
40 ἐξ ἀπάτης εὑρήκασιν ταύτην σχολάζιν, ἐκεῖνον δὲ
ὑπεύθυνον καταστάντες τῷ ἐνκλήματι ἀφ᾿ ὧν
αὐτοὶ ἀνή[ν]εγκαν παρασταθῆναι διὰ τῆς τάξεως.
ἐὰν λέγῃ ὅτι "ὁμολογῖτε ἀναπόγραφον εἶναι τὴν γῆν,"
ἐρ(οῦμεν) ὅτι αὐτὸς τ[ὴ]ν ἄμπελον ἀναπόγραφον εἶπεν.

45 διοριζόμεθα τοίνυν τῆς νέας ἀμπέλου μετρη-
θίσης τότε καὶ ταύτην ἐκ πολλοῦ ὑπῆχθαι καὶ
τὰς ταμειακὰς εἰσφορὰς καταβάλλιν. ἐὰν δὲ καὶ
ὁ κηνσίτωρ ὁ ἀποσταλεὶς ἐκμετρήσας εὕρῃ τι
      ο-   γ
[π]λείῳ πλέον φιλεργηθεῖσαν ὑφ' ἡμῶν, οὐ παραι-
50 τούμεθα τότε, καθ' ὁμοιότητα τῆς ἐπαρχίας,
καὶ ἀπογράψασθαι καὶ τὰ εὐσεβῆ τελέσματα
πληροῖτε. ὡς δὲ ἐπιδὴ πονηρὸν ἔθος εἰσάγει

III   καὶ ὡς δηλατορίαν ἄντικρυς ἦν μισοῦσιν οἱ νόμοι
55 καὶ οἱ δεσπόται ἡμῶν,
κέλευσε ἀνόνητον αὐτῷ
τὴν πῖραν γενέσθαι,
ἀργῖν δὲ τὰ ἀντιγραφέντα
ὑπ' αὐτοῦ.

Names of persons, when they occur for the first time, are marked by a horizontal stroke about 1 or 2 cm. long above the name. The only exception is the name of Diocletian, l. 9.

39.   τὴν l. ἦν.

50.   θ in καθ written over ιτ: cf. l. 51 καὶ τὰ ε-.

52.   πληροῖτε l. πληρῶσαι (?).

"False Accusation. Defendants: Dionysius, ex-protector and Ammonius, beneficiarius. Plaintiff: Dioscorus or rather his son Macrobius.

Both the law and your own hatred of evil despise those who lay claim to the property of others and who lay indictments. This then Dioscorus will be shown to have done, and he deserves to be punished as will be clear from what will be set forth. Theon, the father of the aide and brother of Dionysius, while still alive in the reign of Diocletian now numbered among the gods, registered a grant of land in the cleruchy of Nicanor and bought an additional property besides. Being an energetic person he spent great sums in development and set out part of it in vines. The rest of the estate he cleared and brought under cereal cultivation or put into pasturage. Since that time many years have elapsed, and the estate was divided among the sons when their father died. But while Sarapion was still a minor and the new vineyard was as yet undivided(?) while Theon was alive, it happened that this land which was recultivated in vineyard was subjected to survey and became taxable though recorded by the aides without due care, and for this land they pay the military annona to the most sacred fiscus. But Dioscorus, or, as we have just now learned, his son in his father's name brings boldly a downright libel before Your Grace, and though he personally admits that these fields were brought under cultivation by us originally and set out in vineyard, he falsely asserts that they are untaxed and contribute nothing whatsoever to the most sacred fiscus, whereas, as we claim, the vineyard planted by us was not only surveyed by the *censitor* who was sent out later but also was subjected to taxation. He also claimed that the lands granted by them (i. e. by Diocletian and Maximian?) and improved (by us) be surrendered to him—a thing which no law allows. Since then one should not lay claim to other peoples' property whether they rest their claim on very slight foundations or little better, and since the laws do aid those who have toiled hard, and since he, though openly acknowledging that these lands were owned and cultivated by us, has been willing to lodge a libellous indictment, we beg that no change be made, that this suit which they have devised through deceit be quashed, and, since we have established his liability to the charge, that he be brought to trial in accordance with the edict for those very claims which they have made.

If he offers the plea ' You admit that the land was undeclared,' we shall say that it is he himself who makes this claim. Accordingly we maintain that the new vineyard was surveyed at that time and has long been subject to taxation and is now paying the fiscal charges. But even if the *censitor* who was sent and after survey found the vineyard cultivated somewhat more or less (than the amount stated) we do not then, in accordance with the general practice of the province, beg off from making a declaration and paying in full the sacred taxes. And so, since he is introducing a vicious practice and downright libel, which both the law and our lords despise, give your order that this attempt of his prove of no benefit to him, and that the charges brought by him be voided."

1. The restoration ψευδολογεία is highly problematical. For the penalties involved in bringing false accusation see Mommsen, Röm. Strafrecht, pp. 494 f.; Hitzig, Pauly-Wissowa, R. E., s. v. calumnia. Few *protectores* or members of the imperial body guard are known in Egypt (Preisigke, Wörterbuch, III. p. 218). Dionysius is probably the brother of Theon (l. 8), and the latter probably held the same or higher rank than his brother. Possibly both served with distinction during Diocletian's Egyptian campaign and were rewarded with grants of land.

14. νεμηθέντα. The passive is here used with middle force.

17. ἀναμε[ρισμέν]ης. This seems the only possible restoration. In view of the statement that the estate was divided *after* the father's death (l. 14), it is obvious that the copyist has omitted the negative.

19. Cf. the somewhat similar wording in the edict of Tiberius Julius Alexander (OGIS 669) in regard to the survey of the *chora* of the Alexandrians.

20. τοῖς βοηθοῖς. This appears to be the dative of agent. Apparently the aides of the *censitor* are meant.

24. According to Hornickel, Ehren- und Rangprädikate, the term εὐσεβέστατος is only applied to the emperor. It is doubtful if the use of the phrase τὴν σὴν εὐσέβειαν implies an appeal to the emperor direct, but probably indicates a hearing before the prefect. δηλατορίαν. This Latin word appears here for the first time in papyri from Egypt. Its use indicates the growing influence of Roman law.

31. τὰ ὑπ' ἐκίνων δοθέντα. The pronoun may refer to the defendants but in that case we should expect ὑφ' ἡμῶν or τούτων, and it is difficult to understand what grants by the defendants could mean. If the prepositional phrase is construed with καλλιεργηθέντα, it is perhaps less ambiguous but still somewhat difficult. If reference is made to an imperial grant by Diocletian and Maximian, the scribe might be expected to be less vague about it.

33. The penalty for false declaration prescribed by Diocletian is unknown. Tax-collectors were subject to the death penalty for disobedience in their duties (Boak, Etudes de Papyrologie, II, no. 1), and it is probable that the tax-payer who swore to a false return or who evaded payment of taxes suffered a similar penalty.

40-42. ἐκεῖνον probably refers to Macrobius, the son of Dioscorus while αὐτοί refers to both father and son. The attempt to bring Macrobius to trial seems rather halfhearted and is probably mere bluff. Constantine decreed the death penalty for delation (Cod. Th. X. 10, 2 [319]).

43. This line set out in the left margin offers a plea by the plaintiff for which the defendants present a weak rebuttal. In the statement which follows, they seem to admit that there was some collusion with the tax collectors (see Cod. J. XI. 58, 1 for an edict of Constantine in 313 dealing with collusion between owners and susceptores).

120. PETITION

GD 7612   13.5 × 10.5 cm.   6th century

Apparently about half of this document is lost if we may judge from the position of π(αρά). The subject of dispute is not clear. Some one from the plaintiff's village had married a wife from another village and apparently became a leader in raids against his former villagers. The letter seems to be an appeal to the headman of the village to restrain his people from their lawless acts. If no such action is taken, the plaintiffs will act for themselves, apparently without recourse to law or higher authority.

π(αρὰ)

† τὰ γράμμ[ατ]α τῆς ὑμετέρας ἀδελφότητ[ο]ς ἐ[δ]εξ[άμην
βαρέα ῥήματα ὅπερ οὐκ ὀφείλουσι οἱ εἰρηκότες ὑμῖν τὰ
τοια[ῦτα] ιο..[
ὡς πρὸ τριῶν ἐτῶν ἀπέστη ἀπὸ τῆς ἡμῶν κώμης καὶ κατῆλθεν
[...]οτ[
5 καὶ ἔλαβεν γυναῖκα ἐκεῖ καὶ πολλὰ κακὰ ἐποίησεν εἰς τὰ
ἡμέτερα κτή[ματα
ποιμένων, καὶ ἡμεῖς ἐσμέ⟨ν⟩ σοι ὀφείλοντες ζητῆσαι τὰ κακὰ
γεν[όμενα
παρὰ τῶν ἀπὸ τῆς ὑμετέρας κώμης μὴ οὖν ἔτι τὰ τοιαῦτα
γρ[
ἀναγκάσθωμεν τὰ μὴ πρέποντα θεῷ καὶ ἀνθρώπο[ι]ς οἶδα[
τῶν πραγμάτων καὶ πείσῃ ὑμᾶς ὁ δεσπότης θεὸς ὄψιν α[ὐ]τοῦ ο..[
10   θως αυτ( ) δεσπ( ) †

Verso:

†]ἀ[π]όδ[ος τῷ] κυρίῳ Σαραπίῳ[νι] κεφφ πόλεως Κ[
π(αρὰ) Θεοδοσίου †

B. APPOINTMENT OF OFFICIALS

121. OATH OF SURETY

AM 8936   7.5 × 14 cm.   Theadelphia, A. D. 140(?)

The construction of σιτολόγον in l. 1 is uncertain, but it seems that some one is nominating the *sitologos* for the village of Theadelphia and is surety for his appearance and performance of his duties. For a similar oath cf. BGU 581. This, however, is the earliest example of surety for the sitologi, if that is what this document means. According to Oertel (Die Liturgie, *s. v.*) the sitologi did not have a liturgical character until the fourth century when their office assumes a compulsory character similar to that of other liturgies. Unfortunately the condition of the papyrus in ll. 11-15 is such that the reading cannot be determined. Apparently these lines were written by the guarantor. If the reading ἐκ τοῦ συνόλου is correct, it would seem that the person taking the oath assumed unlimited liability.

Dr. Kase, to whom I owe the preliminary transcript, thought that the year of the emperor could be read as γ, but in the present state of the papyrus, nothing can be read at the beginning of the line.

```
. . . . . . . σιτο-
λόγον κώμης Θεα-
δελφείας ὃν [καὶ παραστ]ήσω
ὁπηνίκα ἐὰν [ἐπιζη]τη-
5  θῆ{ς}. ἐὰν δὲ μὴ παρίσ-
[τηται ἐγ]ὼ αὐ[τὸς]
ἐκ[βι]βάσω τὰ πρὸς
αὐτ[ὸ]ν ἐπιζητού-
μενα ἢ ἔνοχος εἴην
10  τῶ [ὅ]ρκω.
. . . . . . εως τοῦ αὐτοῦ
. . . . . . Θεαδελφείας ἐν-
[γνῶμαι Θέ(?)]ωνα ἐκ τοῦ συνόλου
. . . . . καὶ παραστήσω καθὼς
```

15 πρόκειται.

(ἔτους). Αὐτοκράτορος Καίσαρος Τίτου
Α[ἰλίου Ἀδριανοῦ Ἀν]τωνίνου Σεβ-
[αστοῦ Εὐσε]β[οῦς]. Φαρμοῦθι ε′

"I nominate Theon(?) as sitologus for the village of Theadelphia, and I shall produce him whenever he is required. If he is not produced I shall myself provide for the duties required of him or be liable to the consequences of my oath.
I, X son of .... belonging to the same quarter in Theadelphia offer myself as surety for Theon to the extent of my whole property and I shall produce him as stated above. Date."

122. APPOINTMENT OF A POLICEMAN

GD 7933 A   8.0 × 9.4 cm.   4th century

The document is apparently complete, but there may have been some lines lost above the extant portion, although the space above l. 1 is wide enough for a margin.

The policeman Alammon is appointed to special duty: perhaps to guard the lentil-crop, but the reading φακῶν in l. 1 is very uncertain. The appointment is for one month of the first half-year, but since this is special duty, it throws but little light on the question of the policemen's term of office.

On the Egyptian police in general, see Hirschfeld, *Kleine Schriften* 613-623; Hohlwein, *Musée belge* XI (1905) 187 ff, 394 ff, XII (1906) 169 ff; Jouguet, *Vie municipale* 261 ff; Modica, *Contributi papirologici* 281 ff; Oertel, *Die Liturgie* 263 ff; Wilcken, *Grundzüge* 414 ff.

The συστάτης was in charge of liturgical nominations (Wilcken, *Grundzüge* 353, *Chrest.* 403), as was also the γνωστήρ of the tribe (P Lips, 65).

εἰς φυλακίαν φακῶν
Ἀλάμμων Ἀφθονίου
μῆνα ἕνα πρώτης ἐξαμήνου
Θεόδωρος συστάτης ιζ

4. ιζ rather looks like ιξ, but unless it is a numeral denoting the tribe (cf. P Lips 65), it defies explanation.

C. TAXATION

123. Census List

AM 8918   23.7 × 27.9 cm.   Early 1st century

This roll contains portions of three columns and is evidently a list prepared by the officials of the census giving the name of the taxpayer, his parents and his age. It is probable that the list contains the names of citizens of Philadelphia, partly because of the identity of names in P. Princ. I, nos. 1-15, and because the hand is similar to that of P. Princ. I, 1-6.

Vital statistics from this list are of some interest. The average age is 36.4. From the ages of 48 men preserved, 9 lie between 15-19, 7 fall in the twenties, 13 each in the thirties and forties. After the age of 46 there is a rapid falling off. Five lie in the fifties and only one is listed in the sixties. The small number in the twenties is somewhat surprising. Possibly at this age younger sons went elsewhere in search of employment (see P. Princ. 14 for the large number of Philadelphians in Alexandria).

Col. 1

		]μη( )	Τ..μθεω(ς)	L ιε
		]μη( )	Ταμύσθας	L ιε
		]μη( )	τῆς αὐτῆς	L ..
		]μη( )	Πεκήριος	L μβ
5		]μη( )	Ταύριος	L ιδ
	]ας	μη( )	Θερμούθιος	L κδ
ἄλλο(ς) υἱό(ς)		μη( )	τῆς αὐτῆς	L ις
]...		μη( )	Τανετβέ(ως)	L μβ
		]μη( )	Τανετβήουις	L λβ
10 ἄλ]λο(ς) υἱός		μη( )	τῆς αὐτῆς	L κθ
ἄ]λλο(ς) υἱός		μη( )	τῆς αὐτῆς	L κγ
Πε]τεσούχου		μη( )	Σαμβοῦτο(ς)	L ν
ἄλλος] υἱός		μη( )	Ἰσιδώρας	L ιη
]Πανομγέ(ως)		μη( )	Σαμβοῦτο(ς)	L λθ

15   ]ωνίο(υ)   μη( ) Θενατούμιο(ς)   Ꝉ κγ
   ἄλλ]ος υἱός   μη( ) Θακώριος   Ꝉ . .
   ] . μωθέο(υ)   μη( ) Θενατύμιο(ς)   Ꝉ λε
   ]Πετσίριο(ς)   μη( ) Ταύριος   Ꝉ . γ
   ]ημωνο(ς)   μη( ) Τανεκφ(ερῶτος)   [Ꝉ . .]
20]Χαιρήμωνο(ς)   μη( ) Τανέμε(ως)   Ꝉ λβ
         ]το(υ)   μη( ) Ταορσενούφ(ιος)   Ꝉ ν
   ἄλλος] υἱό(ς)   μη( ) τῆς αὐτῆς   Ꝉ με
         ]ο(υ)   μη( ) Ταύριος   Ꝉ λδ
   ]μωνο(ς)   μη( ) Σαμβοῦτο(ς)   Ꝉ με
25]ωνο(ς)   μη( ) Τεροβά[στ]εω(ς)   Ꝉ μβ
          ]ς   μη( ) Τελύτιος   Ꝉ με
         ]ο(ς)   μη( ) Σαμβοῦτο(ς)   Ꝉ μβ
        ]μη( ) Ταρεώτιδ(ος)   Ꝉ λγ
          ]ς   μη( ) Ταγῶτας   Ꝉ κα
30   'Απύ]γχιος
31-34 traces of letters
35   ]ατο(ς)   μη( ) Θεοβ . . . .
36-7 traces of letters

Col. 2

. . . . ν   A . . . .   μη( ) Διονυσίας   Ꝉ . .
. . . . κε   Τυριου   μη( ) Τανούβιος   Ꝉ . .
Φα . . υς   N . . . .   μη( ) Βερῶτος   Ꝉ . .
'Οννῶφρις   Ψοσνέ(ως)   μη( ) Ταγώτι(ος)   Ꝉ λγ
5 Πτολλαῦς   Φίμωνο(ς)   μη( ) Κλεοπάτρ(ας)   Ꝉ μϛ
Φίμων   υἱός   μη( ) Θασεῖτος   Ꝉ ιθ
Πετεῦς   ἄλλο(ς) υἱό(ς)   μη( ) τῆς αὐτῆς   Ꝉ ιε
'Ανουβᾶς   Φίλβωνο(ς)   μη( ) Κλεοπάτρ(ας)   Ꝉ μγ
Πετεῆς   Πετεῆτος   μη( ) Τασῶτο(ς)   Ꝉ νδ
10 Νεκφερῶς   υἱός   μη( ) Σαμβοῦτος   Ꝉ κγ
'Αρητᾶς   'Ηρακλήο(υ)   μη( ) Ταπεῦτος   Ꝉ
Πεβῶς   ἀδελφός   μη( ) τῆς αὐτῆς   Ꝉ
Πετεῦρις   Πετσίρ(ιος)   μη( ) Θασεῦτος   Ꝉ νη
Κολλαῦθ(ος)   Ψενατύμιο(ς)   μη( ) Τεροβάστ(εως)   Ꝉ λη

15 Κολλαῦθος	ἀδελφός	μη( ) τῆς αὐτῆς	Ⳑ λε
Φέμις	Φεμίστο(ν)	μη( ) Τεφορσεῦτο(ς)	Ⳑ λα
Φέμις	Πετσίριο(ς)	μη( ) Ταύριος	Ⳑ μς
Παθρῆς	Ἡρακλέους	μη( ) Τανεμγέω(ς)	Ⳑ με
Ἡρακλῆς	Πετεύχο(ν)	μη( ) Θεναμούν(ιος)	Ⳑ μθ
20 Πολλῶς	υἱός	μη( ) Ταπετσίριος	Ⳑ κε
Πετσῖρις	ἄλλο(ς) υἱό(ς)	μη( ) τῆς αὐτῆς	Ⳑ ιζ
Ὧρος	Νεκφ(ερῶτος)	μη( ) Τααρμώτιδος	Ⳑ λβ
Ἑρμᾶς	Σαμβᾶτος	μη( ) Θαυρείο(ν)	Ⳑ
Πανετβ(υς)	προγ( ) Νεκφ(ερῶτος) μη( ) Θαύριος		Ⳑ με
25 Ἀρτέμων	Σαμβαθίω(νος) μη( ) Θερμουθ(αρίου)		Ⳑ ξ
Ὡρίων	Ἀρτέμ(ωνος)	μη( ) Θερμώθιος	Ⳑ λα
Παγκράτης	ν(εωτέρου) Ἀρτέμωνος μη( ) Τανομγ(έως)		Ⳑ ις
Πετεαρπ..	Παβοντῶ(τος)	μη( ) Ταγῶτος	Ⳑ νβ
Π......	Ἄμμωνο(ς)	μη( ) Θερμουθ(αρίου)	Ⳑ λα

30-33 traces

Col. 3

Λαλ... [

Μυσθᾶς [

Νεκφεραῦς Ιο[

Μεσουῆρις Π[

5 Παποντῶς Πε...[

Ὀνήσιμος Ἀπελλ[

Ἐσοῦρις Ξένωνος[

Πανετβῆος υἱὸς[

Πανετβῆο(ς) Ἀμούτι(ος)[

10 Αρσ( ) Ἀρφαῆσις Ὀλυμ[πίου

Ἀπολλώνιο(ς)[

Ἀρατρῆς Ψενοσόρ[εως

Ἄδραστος Ἡρακλή(ους) μ[η( )

Ἀρμιεῦς υἱός   μ[η( )

15 Σισόις Πετσίρις   μ[η( )

     vacat

γίνον(ται) ἀπὸ τῶν

. . . .

καὶ τω.... συροι
...τη( ) λ.........
20 Ἡρακλει( ) μερίδος
Ἀρνώθης Καρᾶτος
Πετεσοῦχος Ἀρ[μιύ]σιος
Ψενοβάστις Σισόϊτ(ος)
Σισόϊς υἱός μη( ) Τε
25 Σισόϊς ἄλλο(ς) υἱό(ς) μη( ) τ[ῆς αὐτῆς]
Σισόϊς ἄλλο(ς) υἱό(ς) μη( ) τῆς αὐτῆς
Πτολεμαῖος ....
28-30 traces of three more lines.

Col. 3. 16. Unfortunately the heading which apparently stood here to indicate the subject matter of the following list is indecipherable.

124. OFFICIAL REPORT

GD 7739   12.7 × 17.5 cm.   130/131 A. D.

This document written in clear semi-uncials is complete except at the bottom. In some lines the letters have been exposed to sand blasts and the restoration is problematical. Since metropolitans paid a poll-tax of 20 dr. and villagers 40 dr. in the Fayum, the question of status was important, and the preparations for the census of 132 were doubtless under way. Certain citizens had been registered as metropolitans until the 15th year of Hadrian but apparently they had been unable to prove their right to this classification in proceedings held before the strategus. It is not quite clear what the village secretary of Pterophorusville had to do with the matter. Apparently he had sought to classify them as villagers from the 12th year and when they protested that this registration was false the case came before the strategus of Polemon for decision.

ἐκ λαο[γρα]φίας [κε]φάλαιο(ν) ταμειῶν
ις (ἔτους) Ἀ[δριαν]οῦ [Καί]σαρος τοῦ κυρίου
πρὸ [ὀλίγου χρόν]ο[υ] μεταβλειθείσης
ὑπὸ Π[.......]ου καὶ Μάρωνος γενομένω(ν)
5 γραμματέω(ν) μητροπόλεως μεθ᾽ ἑ-

τερα   κολλ(ήματα) ρμς´ ρμζ´
τῶν ὑπο‖γο‖γεγραμμένων ἀνδρῶν
ἕως ιε (ἔτους) ᾿Αδριανοῦ Καίσαρος τοῦ κυρίου
ἐν μητροπολείταις ἀναγεγραμμένων
10 καὶ κατ᾿ ὑπομνηματισμοὺ⟨ς⟩ ᾿Ανδρο-
μάχου στρατηγοῦ Πολέμωνος
μερίδος προσενεγκαμένων
μὴ δύν[α]σθαι τὸ ἴδιον γένος ἀπο-
δῖξαι ὑπὸ τοῦ κωμογραμματέως
15 Πτεροφόρου ἐποικίου κωμητικὰ
παρα[λελογ]ι[σ]μένων ἔτι ἀπὸ ιβ (ἔτους)
[᾿Α]δριανοῦ τοῦ [κυρί]ου ἕως ἐντεῦθεν
[τὰ δὲ ὀνόματα ὑπ]οτίθεται
[. . . . . . . ᾿Ισ]χυρίωνος τοῦ [Δ]ιοδώρου
. . . .

"Summary of the quaestors from the poll-tax roll made in the 16th year of Hadrian Caesar and lord which had been recorded some time ago by *x* and Maron, former metropolitan secretaries. Following other entries in columns 146 and 147.

Subjoined are the names of those registered as metropolitans until the 15th year of Hadrian reported in the memoranda of Andromachus, strategus of Polemon, as unable to prove their personal status (when they claimed that they had been wrongly assessed(?)) for village taxes by the secretary of the hamlet of Pterophorus from the 12th year of Hadrian until that time. The names are as follows: X son of Ischyrion son of Diodorus."

1. ταμειων. This word should probably be accented ταμειῶν and taken as depending on κεφάλαιον or λαογραφίας. These treasurers thus appear to keep the records of the poll-tax payers and revise them from year to year. They also probably receive the poll-tax from the practors, but hitherto there has been no record of them in either capacity (Oertel, Liturgie, 309). The ταμίας τῶν πολιτικῶν is a municipal officer who appears in the third century (P. O. 55, 1104; BGU. 934).

4. The metropolitan scribes were regularly two in number (Oertel, op. cit. 160; P. Cornell 16). The first mentioned might be restored as Ptolemaeus. Neither he nor Maron is known in this capacity before.

3. μεταβληθείσης. For the meaning 'record' probably with the implication of changing a previous record cf. P. Amh. 68.

16. Dr. Goodrich suggests this restoration which fits the space and the traces of the letters.

125. TAXES ON GARDEN LAND

GD 7626   11 × 9 cm.   Theadelphia(?), A. D. 146

In BGU 1897, l. 28, the elder Athenarion, daughter of [. . . . .]δ ( ) paid the eight-drachma tax on vineyards at Theadelphia in A. D. 166.

For this reason the tentative restoration of Theadelphia is made at the beginning of line 5.

This receipt follows the usual pattern of those for taxes on garden land (see P. Ryl. p. 253 ff., Wallace, Taxation in Roman Egypt, 47 ff.).

Ἔτους ἐνάτου Αὐτοκράτορος Καίσαρος
Τίτου Αἰλίου Ἀδριανοῦ Ἀντωνίνου Σεβασ[το]ῦ Εὐσεβοῦς
Τῦβι ζ διέγρα(ψε) δι(ὰ) Ζωσί(μου) καὶ μετόχ(ων) πρακ(τόρων)
    ἀργ(υρικῶν)
Ἀθηνάριο(ν) πρεσβ(υτέρα) Ἡρώιδο(ς) εἰδῶν ὀγδόου ἔτους
5 [Θεαδ(ελφίας)] ἀμπ(έλου) χα(λκοῦ) Ἀβυμ ναυ[(βίου)] ρκ
    [π(ρ)ο(σδιαγραφομένων)] φιε γ(ίνονται) Ἀγ[οε]
π[....]χ[....]..[....][ὀκταδράχμου] σπον[δῆς Διονύσ]ου
    ἀργυρίων
δραχμὰς ὀκτώι (γίνονται) ∫η π(ρ)ο(σδιαγραφομένων) Ϲϲχᵝ καὶ
    η εἰς
ἀρί[θ(μησιν)] Μεσορὴ [εἰ]δῶ(ν) ὀγδόου <ἔτους> ἀμπ(έλου)
    χα(λκοῦ) ἀνμ π(αραδείσου) φο
ν[αυβ(ίου)?ε (γίνονται)] Ἀβρε π(ρ)ο(σδιαγραφομένων)τκ
    ἐπαρ(ουρίου) αν π(ρ)ο(σδιαγραφομένων) ρι
    κ[ολ(λύβου)] ξε κή
10 (ὀκταδράχμου) ἀργ(υρίου) (δραχμαὶ) δυο (γίνονται) ∫ β καὶ
    προσδ(ιαγροφόμενα)

"The 9th year of Hadrian. Tybi 7th. The elder Athenarión, daughter of Herois has paid the garden taxes for the 8th year at Theadelphia to Zosimus and his associates in collecting taxes in silver, for vineyard 2,440 dr. in bronze, for naubion 120 dr. for supplementary fees 515 dr. Total 3,075 dr. ..... for the 8-dr. as a gratuity of Dionysus 8 dr. in silver. Supplementary fee 3 ob. 6 chalci. Also on the 8th for the account of Mesore for the garden taxes of the 8th year, for vineyard 1440 dr. in bronze, for garden 570 dr., for naubion 95 dr. Total 2,105 dr. Supplementary fee 320 dr. (error for 420 dr.?), for eparourion 1,400 dr., supplement 100 dr., for exchange 65 dr., on the 28th, for the 8-drachma tax in silver 2 dr. and supplementary charges."

5. In receipts for payments in copper drachmae it is usual for χα(λκοῦ) to be prefixed before each payment, but in this document it appears before the first item only.

6. Normally the charge for kollybos, in this case 50 copper dr., should follow the total given at the end of 1.5, but the initial letter seems to be pi. Possibly παρα(δείσου) should be restored, but if so, there is not room for this, its supplementary charge, exchange and total. The reading of the last word in the line is very uncertain. We should expect ἀργυρίου, but the very cursive script looks like ἀργ. κωμ. The supplementary charge on the 8-dr. tax should be 3 ob. Here the receipt must be included.

9. The naubion would normally be a twentieth of the preceding total of 2010 dr., or 100 dr. The supplement should be 420 dr. instead of 320, but the traces of the letter seem clearly to indicate *tau*. At the end of the line a total is expected, but the last two letters apparently indicate the date on which the 8-dr. tax was paid.

10. Since the 8-dr. tax had already been paid in full, this instalment of 2 dr. is unintelligible unless it represents either arrears or a quarterly instalment for the next quadrennium (see Wallace, Taxation, p. 62 f.)

126. OFFICIAL LETTER

GD 7935 B   15.1 × 7.7 cm.   ca. A. D. 150

The eclogistes seems to have been active in the Fayum during the age of the Antonines since most of the documents from the second century belong to this period. Possibly the imperial government in its need of revenue demanded greater vigilance in the collection of taxes.

For the activities of the exetastes see Oertel, Liturgie, 308, Wallace, Taxation, 309. The earliest mention of the exetastes occurs in P. Lond. 1177 (A. D. 113). This document indicates a college of two at Arsinoe drawn from citizens of high standing in the community. The specialized ἐξετασταὶ εἰδῶν appear here for the first time. For the importance of the exetastes in collecting the tax on fullers and dyers see P. Teb. 287.

> Διόφαντος κοσμητεύσας καὶ ['Ήρ]ας ἀρχιερατεύσ-
> ας τῆς Εὐεργτίδεων πόλεως ἐξετασταὶ εἰδῶν
> Ἰ[σ]χυρίωνι τῷ καὶ Διοσκόρῳ Κόσμου χαίρειν.
> ἐν τοῖς ἀναπεμφθεῖσι ὑπὸ τοῦ τοῦ ν[ομοῦ] ἐγλογι-
> 5 στοῦ εἰς ἐξέτασιν εἴδεσιν τῆς διοικήσεως [....]πλ.
> καὶ δηλοῦται ἐωνῆσθαί σε παρὰ Ἡ[ρωνί]νου [τοῦ κ(αὶ)]
> Δημ[οσ]θένους Νι[κο]μήδεως ἀφ' [ὧν παρε]χωρή-
> θη (ἀρουρῶν) ϛ εἰς ἀμπ[έλ]ου φυτείαν [.....]οικω
> . . . . .

" Diophantus excosmete and Heras former chief priest of Ptolemias Euergetis, examiners of the garden taxes, greet Ischyrion also called Dioscursus son of Cosmus. In the report of the garden taxes of the administration sent up by the auditor of the nome . . . . it is also shown that that you have purchased from Heroninus also called Demosthenes son of Nicomedes for the planting of a vineyard from the six arouras transferred . . . .

127. REPORT OF λαογράφοι

GD 7926 B   10.9 × 12.6 cm.   159/160

The λαογράφοι report concerning the κατ' ἄνδρα ἀπογραφή, which seems to have been required in addition to the κατ' οἰκίαν ἀπογραφή. A list of the published ἀπογραφαὶ κατ' οἰκίαν is given by Wallace, *Taxation*, 392 ff. For the function of the λαογράφοι in verifying the census, cf. Oertel, *Die Liturgie* 179; Wallace, *Taxation*, ch. VII and especially p. 396.

For the officials charged with the conveyance of records to Alexandria, see P. Amh. 69; P. Flor. 358; P. Ryl. 83.

Ζωί[λω κ]αὶ Τρύφωνι καὶ τοῖς
σὺν αὐτοῖ[s] προχειρισθ(εῖσι) π[ρ]ὸς παρά-
λημψιν καὶ κατακομιδὴν βιβλί-
ων πε[μπ]ομένων εἰς 'Αλεξάνδρειαν
5 τῷ τοῦ νομοῦ ἐγλογιστῇ
παρὰ [...]τιώνιος καὶ 'Αρσύθμεως
καὶ τῶ[ν ἄλ]λων λαογράφω(ν) κώμη(s) Θεαδελφ(είας)
κατεχωρίσαμεν ὑμεῖν κατ' ἄνδρα
ἀπογρ(αφὴν) τῶν ἀπογραψαμένω(ν) ἡμεῖν
10 πρὸς τὴν τοῦ κγ (ἔτους) Αἰλίου
'Αντωνίνου κατ' οἰκί(αν) ἀπογρ(αφὴν). ἡ συν-
τεθεῖσα ἀκολουθ(εῖ) τοῖς ἐπιδοθ(εῖσιν)
ἡμεῖν κολλήμασι Ζώιλος ...

"To Zoilus and Tryphon and their associates chosen for the receipt and conveyance of reports sent to Alexandria to the auditor of the nome from ... tion, Harsythmis and other census-takers of the village of Philadelphia. We have filed with you the census return of men listed by us in the house-to-house census of the 23rd year of Antoninus. The supplement follows the rolls handed in by us: Zoilus ....."

128. REPORT OF VILLAGE SCRIBE

GD 7926c   7.5 × 7.5 cm.   *post* 163/4 A. D.

This document is complete on top and right side. Not much has been lost on the left, and apparently three or four letters are missing at the beginning of lines.

The office of *plerotes* has hitherto been known from a very fragmentary document (P. Fay. 23), where some one is named to this liturgy for a village in the Fayum, and from P. Hamb. 59 (A. D. 138) where the secretary of the *plerotae* reports that all public and usiac land in the village of Philadelphia has been flooded and seeded by December 15. In the present document the secretary of the village of Theadelphia reports to the board of *plerotae* the names of tenants who had sublet from Heron. The *plerotae* hold a public liturgy in the second century and their duties seem to be somewhat that of the village secretary in controlling the leasing of land (Cf. Berl. Leihgabe 7 where the village secretary of Lagis and Tricomia reports on vacant leaseholds and those assigned to care for them). The meaning of the word implies that the *plerotae* saw to it that the public land was fully leased, properly flooded, and sown in good season. In the third century the *pragmatikos* at Oxyrhynchus may have discharged the same function (P. O. 899, A. D. 200).

> ... .. πληρώτῃ καὶ τοῖς σὺν αὐτῷ
> [παρ]ὰ Ḥ[....]νος κωμογρα(αμματέως) Θεαδελφείας ·
> [ἐπιζ]ητοῦσι ὑμεῖν κατ᾽ ἄνδρα τῶν γεωργ-
> [ῶν τῶν] ἐν πιττακίῳ Ἥρωνος Μυσ-
> 5 [θαρίωνο]ς δηλῶ τοὺς ὑπογεγραμμέ-
> [νους τ]ετ[ά]χθαι διὰ τῆς μεταβληθείσης
> [.... ὑ]πὸ τοῦ πρὸ ἐμοῦ κωμογρ(αμματέως) Σαρα-
> [πίω]νος πρὸς τὸ γ (ἔτους) Ἀντωνίνου καὶ
> [Οὐήρο]υ τῶν Κ[υρ]ίων Σεβαστῶν δια-
> 10 [γραφῆς(?)] .... ὡς ὀφείλει κτλ.

" To X and his associates, *plerotae*, from Heron(?), village-secretary of Theadelphia. In answer to your request for the individual names of the tenants on the assignment of Heron, son of Mystharion, I report that the following were appointed there according to the report registered by my predecessor Sarapion in the 3rd year of Antoninus and Verus."

1. Traces of two letters may be seen about the small wormhole to the left of πληρώτῃ, and the surface of the papyrus at the beginning of the line shows no trace of ink. However it is unlikely that the first line was indented and the name of the *plerotes* may have stood in the lost portion on the left. If so, the name was a short one.

2. The name of the village scribe may be restored as Heron. Ploution was in office 158-161 (Berlin Leihgabe 5; Gr. Texte 4). Sarapion (see lines 7-8) was in office in 163, and Heron is his immediate successor, probably not much later than 163.

Sarapion who held office under Trajan (P. Iand. 31) may have been the grandfather of the secretary in 163.

4. πιττακίῳ. This term in connection with leases of public land is discussed by Kalén, Berlin Leihgabe 22 (A. D. 155). In this document Heron had evidently taken a large allotment of public land and sublet it to various tenants. The use of τετάχθαι in line 6 may imply that the sublease was by no means voluntary. Does the present report imply that these tenants had fled their allotments?

6. μεταβληθείσης. See no. 124 and P. Amh. 68 for the meaning 'register.' Here the word is probably to be construed with διαγραφῆς (1. 9) but possibly we should restore ἀπο(γραφῆς) at the beginning of 1. 7 and make a different restoration at the beginning of 1. 10.

129. Census Declaration

GD 7928 B   8 × 12 cm.   A. D. 188/9

Since M. Aurelius Papirius Dionysius, prefect in 187/8 (P. O. 1110), ordered a census for the current 28th year, he was followed immediately by Tineius Demetrius under whom the census was taken in the Fayum in accordance with the edict of his predecessor. Hitherto Tineius had been known only from a document dated August, 190 (P. Teb. 336, cf. Reinmuth, Prefects of Egypt, p. 137).

These declarations were pasted together to form a roll. The ends of lines of the document preceding this are preserved, but very little is worth recording. The name of Tineius Demetrius is preserved in part in 1. 3, and possibly the name of his predecessor in 1. 8 where Αὐρηλίου is read.

Col. 2

```
   [Φ]ανομγέω[ς                                    ]
   [Πα]ήσιος μ(ητρὸς)[          ]μου μετὰ
   [τοῦ κ]υρίου Παν .. ου Ἑρμίου
   [          ]κατὰ τὰ κελενσθ(έντα)
 5 [ὑ]πὸ Τινηίου Δημητρίου
   [τοῦ] λαμπ(ροτάτου) ἡγεμόνος ἀπὸ
   [τοῦ] προστ(άγματος) τοῦ διελθ(όντος) κη (ἔτους)
   [κα]τ' οἰκ(ίαν) ἀπογρ(αφὴν) τὰ ὑπάρχ(οντά)
   [μοι περὶ τὴν κώμην] Βουβαστ( )
10 ... οἰκ(ίαν) καὶ αὐλ(ήν)
   [....]σὺν ἄλ[λοις          ]αὐτῆς...
   [....]πτουντι Ἕλλου (ἐτῶν) λβ
```

[. . . .]ναρις θυγ(ατ   ) αὐτοῦ ἐξε
[. . . .]Ἴσιδι θυγ(ατ   )   ὡς (ἐτῶν) ιγ
15 [. . . . .] ὡς (ἐτῶν)ι
[ὑπάρ]χ(οντα) δέ μοι καὶ Πεβῶτι
[. . . .]η( ) (πρότερον) Ταποντῶτος
[Πα]ήσιος καὶ οἰκ(ία) καὶ τόπ(ος)
[καὶ] ὀμνύω τὴν Αὐρηλίου
20 [Κομ]μόδου Ἀντωνείνου
[Καίσα]ρος τοῦ κυρίου
[τύχην.]

130. REPORT OF TAX-COLLECTORS

GD 7654   10 × 11.5 cm.   A. D. 198-209

Since payments are made in multiples of four drachmae, this is
apparently a report of the collectors of poll-tax. Apparently one
column at least preceded this. A village called Thonis is known in
the Oxyrhynchite nome. Whether Nedymos is a personal name or
that of a castellum cannot be determined since all traces of writing
have disappeared before the initial letter. An ἐποίκιον Νηδ(ύμου) is
known in the Fayum (P. Princeton 13). Since the collectors of poll-tax
did not operate in different nomes, it is probable that Nedymos is a
personal name, but it is uncertain what function he and Horion had in
relation to the practors.

Ἀτρῆς Νεχθώτου	∫ ις
Εὐσωφύριος υἱὸς Πέκω[τος]	∫ ις
Πετεσθεῦς υἱὸς Πενεχθ[ερ]ώτου	∫ ις
Σαραπίων υἱὸς Πενεχθ[ερώτ]ου	∫ ιβ
5 Πετεσθεῦς Νεχθώτ[ου]	∫ ιβ
Νεχθώτης Νεχθώτου	∫ ιβ
Ὀρσενοῦφις Εὐσωφυρίου	∫ ιβ
Νεχθώτης Ψευδερή[το]υ	∫ ιβ
Ταυρεῖνος Παχούμιος	∫ μ
10 Ὧρος Ὥρου	∫ ιβ
Φᾶφις Φάφιος	∫ ιβ

ἐπὶ τὸ α(ὐτὸ) ∫ χνς [ἀπὸ μηνὸς   ]

ἄχρι μηνὸς Φαρ[μοῦθι   ἔτους   ]

Αὐτοκρατόρων Καισάρων Λουκίου Σεπτιμ[ίου]

15 Σεουήρου Εὐσεβοῦς Περτίνακ[ος 'Α]ραβικοῦ 'Αδι[αβηνικοῦ]

Παρθικοῦ μεγίστου καὶ Μάρκ[ου] Αὐρηλίου 'Αντ[ωνίνου]

Εὐσεβοῦς Σεβαστῶν[   ]

Νεκθερ(ῶς) Πιλάτ(ου) καὶ 'Οἰνο[. . . . .] καὶ Φιλοπ.[πράκτορες]

ἀργυ(ρικῶν) κώμης Θωνι[. . . . .] Νηδύμ(ου)

20 'Ωρίωνος καὶ 'Ονθον[

131. Taxes on Catoecic Land

GD 7732   14.8 × 26.5 cm.   A. D. 197

Special taxes, the τελη καταλοχισμῶν, were exacted on the transfer of catoecic land. According to the gnomon (P. Iand. 137) the tax paid by men on arable land was 4 dr., by women 8 dr. per ar. The tax paid by Perigeneia on 26½ ar. amounted to 212 dr. including gratuities. From the receipt it appears that she owed in all 233 dr. with gratuities. The difference of 21 dr. is evidently the 10% tax on sales of land (Wallace, Taxation, pp. 227 f.). It is also evident that she had to pay interest on arrears. So in the Tax Rolls from Karanis published by Youtie interest is exacted on loans and the purchase of property (Index, p. 141, s. v. Interest). For a discussion of σπονδή see Wallace, op. cit. s. v.

Nilus and his partner held the contract for several nomes. In P. Tebt. 357 (Wilcken, Chrestomathie 372) they are called the collectors for the Arsinoite and other nomes. Wilcken's suggestion that prominence is given to the nome where the receipt is issued is confirmed by the present document. Some six years later Sarapammon is named alone (P. Harrer 77) and Nilus had either died or dropped from the firm.

Νεῖλος καὶ Σαραπάμμων δημοσιῶναι

καταλοχ(ισμῶν) 'Οξυρυνχ(ίτου) καὶ ἄλλων νομῶ(ν)

διὰ Νεπωτιανοῦ τοῦ καὶ 'Απολλωνίο[υ πραγ(ματεύτου)

Περιγενείᾳ αὐτῇ θυγατρὶ Μάρκου [4 ll.]

5 Πεσοῦρος μητρ(ὸς) Δημητρίας Σαραποδ[ώρου]

διὰ 'Απολλωνίου το[ῦ κ]αὶ Διδύμου Ἀ[   ]
τοῦ Διοσκόρου Σωσικλῆ τοῦ Καλᾶ χαίρειν.
διέγρ(αψας) ἡμῖν τέλ(η) περὶ Πέλα ἐκ τ(ῶν)
Διοδώρου τοῦ Δημοκράτου κατ(οικικῶν) (ἀρουρῶν) κϛ ∠'
10 τοῦ προκα⟨τέ⟩χω(ντος) Πανέτβη .... ηριος
μητρ(ὸς) Καλλαυχίας ἀπὸ Πέλα διὰ τοῦ
καταλογ(είου) τῷ διελη(λυθότι) γ (ἔτει) Παχῶν τὰς
(δραχμὰς) ριε λοι(πὰς) σὺν σπονδ(αῖς) ἐν χρήσ(ει) δραχ(μὰς)
ἑκατὸν δεκαοκτώ. (γίνονται) (δραχμαὶ) ριη.
15 (ἔτους) δ Αὐτοκράτορος Καίσαρος Λουκίου
Σεπτιμίου Σεουήρου Εὐσεβοῦς Περτίνακος
Σε̣[β]αστοῦ 'Αραβικοῦ 'Αδιαβηνικοῦ. Φαμενὼ[θ] κ[ ]

"Nilus and Sarapammon, farmers of the land-transfer tax for the Oxyrhynchite and other nomes, represented by their agent Nepotianus also called Apollonius, greet Perigeneia, daughter of Marcus also called Pesourus and Demetria whose father was Sarapodorus, represented by Apollonius also called Didymus A.... son of Dioscorus Sosicles son of Calas. You have paid the transfer tax on 26½ ar. of catoecic land near Pela in the allotment of Diodorus son of Democrates formerly owned by Panetbes son of ....erius and Callauchia of Pela through the registry office for the preceding year in Pachon to the amount of 115 dr. Balance including gratuity remaining on interest 118 dr. Total 118 dr. Date."

132. REPORT OF THE TAX OVERSEERS

AM 11242   7 × 20 cm.   2nd century

Top and left margins preserved. Broken at right and bottom. Probably part of a roll containing similar reports as the heading of this column implies a preceding column. In most cases the report seems to cover the period from Thoth to Payni but ll. 13 and 33 show different periods. The nature of the report is not clear. Apparently each special tax is reported or audited. Thus in l. 9 the overseers of the tax on Syrian wool and on shepherds use a formula seemingly repeated with slight variation in almost every other tax. There appears to be no other parallel to this formula at present known and it is so far abbreviated that the restoration is not certain. υπ( ), written as υ', may be restored in various ways, but evidently some noun or a verb in the infinitive mood to balance εἶναι is required. Areio—seems to be a personal name which recurs several times but his connection with the account is unknown, unless he had sublet the farming of the tax. The tax on Syrian wool and the Egyptian drug, whatever that may be, are new. The ferrymen of Phemeo( ) apparently have some form of monopoly. The following entries are listed under geographic headings but the nature of the tax cannot be determined. The village of Psenephtha is unknown. Possibly the name is a variant of Senepta at Oxyrhynchus. Phenyletheines and the city of Isis are not recorded elsewhere. The Seven Villages have no connection with the nome Heptacomia. The names in ll. 29 and 31 are also unknown. In line 34 the entry deals with a φόρος but the traces of letters cannot be identified with any of the φόροι listed by Wallace, Taxation in Roman Egypt.

καὶ Μένου Ὥρου Πμώχ[ιος   ]
καὶ Ὥρου Ἕρμου ἀπὸ Ψω[
καὶ τοὺς ʃ ὁμοί(ως) Π.εσω[
καὶ μετοχ( ) καὶ Ὥρου Ἐρ[
5 Πμώχιος ἐν συγκολ( ) λ. [
ἐπιτηρήσεως τελωνικῶν[
ἐπιτηρεθέντων ἀπὸ Θὼθ [ἕως
ἐρίων συρικῶν καὶ ποιμέν[ων
δηλ(ωθέντων) ὑπ( ) καὶ εἶναι λογο( ) Ἀρειο( )[
10 καὶ ....ειφεν συγκολ( )[
φαρμάκου Αἰγύπτου[
    δηλ( ) ὑπ( ) καὶ εἶναι λογ( ) Ἀρει[
    Ἡρακλη( ) ἀπὸ Θὼθ ἕως Φ[
    Ευθ( ) Τερφιλ( ) ..ευχου[
15 ἀρτυματοπωλ( )[
    .οληετων πρὸ τ[
πραθμίδων Φεμεω[
    Ηκαλαχει καὶ Ψαμεουλ[
    δηλ( ) εἶναι Ἀρειο( ) Ἡρα[ἀπὸ]
20   Θὼθ ἕως Παῦνι[
Ψενέφθα δηλ( ) εἶναι λ[ογο( )
    ἀπὸ Θὼθ ἕως Παῦνι[
Φηνυλεθείνεως δηλ ( ) ὑπ( )[καὶ εἶναι λογο( )
    λθ΄΄ ἀπὸ Θὼθ ἕως[

25 Ἴσιδος πόλεως δηλ( ) [εἶναι λογο( )
    Παπέσκο(υ) ἀπὸ Θὼθ ἕως[
  Ἑπτὰ κώμας Τειχωε( ) |
    ... νυριο(υ) ἀπὸ [Θὼθ ἕως
  Κοινοτηθερατ[
30   Πεπτεύρου ἀπὸ Θὼθ [ἕως
  .δυσωνδ( ) Ἀθα[
    Ἰσχυρίω(νος) Εὐθο[
    ἀπὸ Μεχεὶρ ἕ[ως
  φόρου ....εδ.ρου[

3. The sign following τοὺς may perhaps be resolved as αὐτοὺς.

    The reference to Syrian wool and shepherds in the same line might imply that this wool was produced in Egypt rather than imported. For the activity of Apollonius in raising Milesian wool in the Fayum, see Préaux, L'economie royale des Lagides, 107, 220.

11. The use of the singular need not necessarily imply a tax on a single drug, although such an interpretation is not to be ruled out. No special Egyptian drug is known, and it is unlikely that the prescription given by Galen (XIII, p. 643, Kühn) was the object of a special tax.

15. ἀρτυματοπῶλ(αι). The tax on dealers in condiments is found in BGU. 1087, PO. 1517.

17. πραθμίδων. Cf. BGU. 1188. The form προθ(μοφυλακία) is found in P. Ryl. 185, 193.

25. The use of πόλις does not imply a city. The Oxyrhynchite village Ἴσιον or Ἰσεῖον is well known but it is never called a city.

29-31. Probably the names of villages stand at the beginning of these lines.

34. If this line begins with φόρος, a new series of entries begins at this point.

133. RECEIPT

GD 7738   10.5 × 26 cm.   A. D. 303

The names of the bankers, high officials of the municipality of Oxyrhynchus, are not recorded elsewhere. Management of the public bank was an important duty and called for considerable talent and wealth. At this time banking evidently obtained higher social standing in the community through the position of the public bankers.

    Αὐρήλιοι [Π]τολμίω(ν) ἐξηγητὴς καὶ
    Ἡρα[κλ]ειαν[ὸ]ς ὁ καὶ Μωρίων ἀρχιε-

ρεῦ[s ἀ]μφό[τ]εροι βουλευταὶ τῆς λαμ(πρᾶς)
καὶ [λ]αμπρο(τάτης) Ὀ[ξυ]ρυγχειτῶν πόλεως
5 δη[μο]σ(ίων) χρημά(των) τραπεζεῖται Αὐρηλία Σ[ι]ντοτόη τῇ καὶ Ἀλειταρείῳ χ(αίρειν)
διέ[γ]ραψας ἡμῖν ἐπὶ τὴν τοῦ νομοῦ
δη[μοσί]α[ν τ]ράπ[ε]ζαν εἰς ἀρίθμη-
σιν[. . . . . το]ῦ μ[ην]ὸς Χοίακ λ ´
10 ὑπ[ὲρ . . . . .]ολίου [ἐ]ποικίω Ταωτρι. .
[. . . . .]s ιθ/ καὶ ιη/
καὶ [ια/ . . . . . . δρ]αχμὰς τρισχει-
λί[ας] (γίνονται δραχμαὶ) Γ
ἔτους [ἐννεακ]αιδεκ[ά]του καὶ (ἔτους) ιη/
15 [τῶν δεσποτῶν] ἡμῶ[ν] Διοκλητιανοῦ
κα[ὶ Μαξιμιανοῦ Σεβα]στ[ῶν καὶ (ἔτους) ια
[Κωνσταντίου καὶ Μαξιμιανοῦ τῶν]
[ἐπιφανεστάτων Καισάρων] Παῦνι ι. ´

After a space of two lines is a further memorandum of two lines which are now quite illegible.

"Aurelius Ptolmio exegete and Aurelius Heraclianus also called Morio chief priest, both senators of the most distinguished city of Oxyrhynchus, managers of the public bank greet Aurelia Sintotoe also called Alitarion. You have paid into the public bank of the nome the sum of 3,000 dr. for the reckoning of the month Choiak on behalf of . . . . in the hamlet of Taotri . . for the 19th year of Diocletian, the 18th year of Maximian and the 11th year of the Caesars. Payni 1(.)."

9. Possibly εἰδῶν, which fits the space, should be restored here. For εἴδη ἀννωνικὰ see Rouillard, L'administration civile, 109, n. 6. The reading λ is quite clear, but it is unusual to find the day of month expressed in this formula.

10. ἐποικίω. Dative used for genitive. The name of the hamlet is otherwise unrecorded.

11. Some designation of the emperors should stand at the beginning of this line.

134. LAND REGISTER

GD 7932   Theadelphia, 4th century

This register consists of two fragments, No. I (30 × 12 cm.) containing two columns, No. II containing the third column. None of the columns is complete and traces of lines are still preserved in each at the bottom. The hand is clear and legible, much more so than the usual official reports. In all cases the abbreviation designating private land is represented by the form ἰδιο( ). Wilcken (Grundzüge, 315) has suggested that this should be expanded as ἰδιω(τικῆς) rather than as ἰδιο(κτήτου) since no example of the latter is known to him from the fourth century. However the consistent use of the form ἰδιο ( ) by this scribe suggests that the latter should be restored.

The chief importance of the register lies in the names which reappear frequently in Theadelphian documents of the fourth century (P. Thead. *passim*). The size of the holdings, varying from two to sixty arouras, indicates the tendency to larger estates characteristic of the period.

Col. 1

κατ᾽ ἄνδρα κωμητικῆς κτήσεως
κώμης Θεαδελφίας ὑπὲρ τῆς δεκάτης
   ἰνδικτίωνος. Ἔστι δὲ

Πανηοῦς Ἱερέως	βασι(λικῆς)σπο(ρίμου)	(ἄρουραι) μα η ιϛ		
5		ἰδιο( )	σπο( )	Ⴆ ϛ d ιϛ
Πᾶσις Νειλάμμωνος	ἰδιο( )	σπο( )	Ⴆ γ η
Σακαῶν Σαταβοῦτος	βασι( )	σπο( )	Ⴆ ιθ η
	ἰδιο( )	σπο( )	[. . . . . . .]

Col. 2

Ψαῶν Ὠρίωνος	βασι( )	σπο( )	Ⴆ λγ d η
	ἰδιο( )	σπο( )	Ⴆ κγ ၓ η ιϛ λο
	βασι( )	ἀσπό(ρου)	Ⴆ β ၓ ιϛ ξο
⁵ᵗⁱ Ἀειὰς Σεράτο(ς) γυνὴ Ὠρίωνος	βασι( ) σπο( )		Ⴆ η d
5 Ὠρίων ἐπίκλην Καγολ Ἥρωνος	βασι( ) ασπ( )		Ⴆ ιβ λο
Ἀλλίων Σαταβοῦτος	βασι( )	σπο( )	Ⴆ ϛ ιο
	ἰδιο( )	σπο( )	Ⴆ ϛ ၓ ιϛ λο
Ἐσοῦρις Ὠρίωνος	βασι( )	[σπο( )	Ⴆ] ι d
	[ἰδιο( )	σπο( )]	Ⴆ ιϛ ၓ η λο

Col. 3

Ἀρείων Διοσκόρου	βασι( )	σπο( )	Ⴆ ε ιϛ
	ἰδιο( )	σφο( )	Ⴆ κα λο
	βασι( )	ἀσπ( )	Ⴆ β ιϛ

		ἰδιο( )	ἀσπο( )	Ꝝ	α	∫	η̄	ις̄	λο̄
5	Ἀτίανα Διοσκόρου	ἰδιο( )	σπο( )	Ꝝ	μδ	d	η̄		
		ἰδιο( )	ἀσπ( )	Ꝝ	γ		η̄	λο̄	
	Σακαῶν Πεμουτίου	ἰδιο( )	σπο( )	Ꝝ	α	d	ῑο		
	Ἀμῖς Παησίου	βασι( )	σπο( )	Ꝝ	α	d	η̄		

2. The tenth indiction gives the only clue to date, i. e. not before A. D. 322, cf. Kase, Papyrus Roll, 25 ff. If Sakaon, son of Satabous, was born ca. A. D. 265-270, this date is probably correct (P. Thead. pp. 25 ff.).

4. It may be noted that the proportion of crown land to private property, as estimated in this fragment, is almost equal. The disappearance of crown land after the fourth century is noted by Wilcken (Grundzüge, 310 f.). It may be observed that very little land is reported as unsown, and evidently the irrigation system was still functioning in this village.

Col. 2. 4. The marginal comment implies that some investigation was demanded in the case of this woman holding crown land. It may be noted that Atiana was taxed only for private property (Col. 3. 5). In the Roman period women could hold crown land on lease but could not be compelled to take such leases.

135. ACCOUNT AND LIST OF NAMES

GD 7666   8 × 18 cm.   4th century

The names on the *verso* have been checked at the left with a slanting bar. The significance of πο( ) on the *recto* is uncertain. It can hardly be explained as ποιμένες. Possibly some sort of a measure as in P. Lond. 1718, where its significance is also obscure.

$$\begin{aligned}
&ὑπερ\ πο(\ )\ φ\ η. \\
&ὑπερ\ (ἀρουρῶν)\ τκη\ πο(\ )\ κγ \\
&ὑπερ\ τῶν\ (ἀρουρῶν)\ ις\ πο(\ )\ α \\
&καὶ\ ὑπερ\ τῶν\ (ἀρουρῶν)\ λ\ πο(\ )\ β. \\
5\ &..\ ριθ//\qquad\qquad\qquad ρκα \\
&................................ \\
&\qquad\qquad πο(\ )\ ις \\
&\qquad\qquad πο\ (\ )\ κγ \\
...\ &ῑο
\end{aligned}$$

1-4. A slanting bar drawn through the final letter in ὑ π ε ρ indicates some sort of abbreviation.

Verso

.. ρουβος Τεβεσείων   μικ[ρός
'Ανοῦφις Εὐλογίου
Μακάριος Κόπιος   μικρ[ός
Τίμαιος Νείλου
5 'Ιούλι[ος 'Αλυ]πίου
. . . .]κοντίου

. . . .

]ν Συριακοῦ
]ος 'Αγάθου
10   'Ι]σάκ
]ις 'Ισάκ
] .. παίου

. . . .

Κωνστάντιος Ορ[
15 [Γ]αῖος Ζωίλου
Πάνος Εἰρηνίου
'Ηρακλῆς Μετάβολος
Παποντῶς Νείλου
κληρ(ονόμοι) Παμουθίου
20 "Απιος Κηπάρου
Σαραπάμμων Κ.[..
Πλουτίων Βελάνο[υ]

136. LAND REGISTER

GD 7980 A   18 × 20 cm.   4-5th century

The document, apparently an official register of land, is of interest because similar registers of this period are unknown. Since right and left margins appear to be original and the only break is at the bottom, it probably formed part of a folio rather than a roll. Since the names of the tax-payers were set out in the left margin, the present leaf begins with the middle of an account on the *recto*, and from the summary in line 4, it may be inferred that five or six entries were to be found on the preceding page under the name of this tax-payer. The account evidently dealt with large landholders. Thus on the *verso*, the incomplete record of the son of Paul shows that he held at least $89\frac{7}{16}$ arouras in different ἐδάφη, but whether on leasehold or as owner is uncertain.

An interesting feature of the register is the fact that only a small percentage of the holdings is taxed. Out of $89\frac{7}{16}$ arouras on the *verso* only $12\frac{1}{2}$ are recorded as paying taxes. Another curious element is the division of each area into three (or two) equal parts. Thus in *recto* ll. 1-3, $1\frac{23}{64}$ ar. are divided into three equal lots each of which is assessed for wheat, barley and flax. The scribe is not always accurate. Thus in *recto* 5-7, $1\frac{3}{4}$ ar. are divided into three lots of $\frac{9}{16}$ ar., leaving $\frac{1}{16}$ ar. unaccounted for, although the calculation of the tax seems to indicate that this sixteenth was divided between the wheat and barley. Similarly in *verso* 1-3, $2\frac{3}{4}$ ar. are divided into lots of $\frac{7}{8}$ ar. with $\frac{1}{8}$ ar. unaccounted for, though again the assessment shows that it was divided between wheat and barley. The equality of division is not rigorously maintained. Thus on the Great Estate $3\frac{1}{8}$ ar. are divided into two lots of 1 and one of $1\frac{1}{8}$ ar., and 5 ar. on the estate of Zeno are divided into two lots of $2\frac{3}{4}$ and $2\frac{1}{4}$ ar. The taxable area bears no relation to the holding on each estate. It is unlikely that the remainder of the property escaped taxation.

Whatever the nature of Diocletian' reform, it is evident that the system of taxation on arable land was little changed from Ptolemaic or Roman times. Land in wheat and barley was taxed at 7 (or 6) artabas per aroura. To this was added a supplement of 1% (actually 10%). This rate, if uniform, was somewhat higher than that imposed earlier on crown land, but higher rates may be found on imperial estates (Wallace, Taxation, p. 11). Land in hay is taxed at 2 artabas of wheat or barley per ar. with a similar supplementary charge. Sometimes the payment in grain is commuted to money at the rate of $\frac{5}{8}$ gold *nomisma*. In *recto* 1, the account neglects $\frac{1}{128}$ in favor of the tax-payer, and apparently there was no supplement exacted when the payment in kind was commuted to money. Incidentally we may assume that price of 2 artabas of wheat at this time was $\frac{5}{8}$ of the *nomisma*. Flax was taxed at rates varying from 14-17 bundles of hemp per **ar.**, with a supplementary tax of 5%.

The supplementary tax of 1% (σὺν ρ) is found elsewhere in Byzantine records (P. Lips. 84; P. Iand. 63; P. Cairo 67, 169; 67, 347;

P. Lond. 1755-57, 1761, P. O. 2022). In the British Museum papyri, which are much later in date, there is also a charge for transport which is lacking here. This supplement is usually identified with the earlier ἑκατοστή, but in the Byzantine period it is evident that the supplement of 1% is a legal fiction and from the calculation of the rate in this document it includes all the various supplements imposed in Roman times in a lump sum which now seems to be fixed at 10% of the tax assessed. Thus in *recto* 2-3 $^{29}\!/_{64}$ ar. in wheat and barley are taxed at 7 art. with a supplement of 1% yielding a total of 3½ art. The actual tax on this area yields $3^{11}\!/_{64}$ art. and the supplement is therefore $^{21}\!/_{64}$ art. or approximately 10%. Two exceptions may be noted: *recto* 6, $^{9}\!/_{16}$ ar. in wheat and barley yield 4½ art. and 4 choenices. The actual tax is $3^{15}\!/_{16}$ art. The supplement (assuming 40 choenices per art.) is $^{53}\!/_{80}$ art., or approximately 13%. However it should be noted that in this entry the scribe has neglected to record $\frac{1}{16}$ ar. and if this area is divided up between the wheat and barley, the supplementary tax is found to be ca. 10%. Similarly in *verso* 2-3 the supplement seems to be 18%, but again ⅛ ar. has been omitted by the scribe, and if this is taken into account, the supplement is approximately 10%. In the case of flax the supplement of 5% imposed on bundles of hemp works out in actual practice with considerable variations (from 5-7%). However when we consider that the scribe is dealing with rather minute fractions of the aroura and that minute fractions of a bundle of flax must have been an absurdity, such variations are to be expected. Apparently fractions less than an eighth were disregarded.

Granting that the supplement in payments of wheat and barley is 10% of the tax, the size of the artaba may be considered. In two cases payments (*verso* 6-7 [probably the same area as 7-8]; 10) correspond exactly with an artaba of 40 choenices. In the other two cases (*recto* 6-7; *verso* 6) where more complicated fractions are involved the artaba works out at a fraction under 56 choenices in the former and 53⅓ choenices in the latter. However the artaba of 40 choenices gives a reasonable approximation to the total tax in all cases, and probably this was the size of the artaba in use.

Recto

1　　　　ἀπὸ (ἀρουρῶν) κθ′ χόρ(του) (ἀρουρῶν) α ϙ ῑō τῆς

[(ἀρουρᾶς)] νο(μίσματος) ⌐ η νο(μίσματα) α η̄ καὶ
ἀπὸ ἐδάφ(ους) Δεπ ( ) ἀ[πὸ (ἀρουρῶν) ..]

2 (ἀρουρῶν) α d ῑο λο̄ ξο̄ ὧν (πυρῷ) (ἄρουραι) d η̄ ῑο ξο̄ ἀνὰ
(πυροῦ ἀρτάβας) ζ σὺν ρ (γίνονται πυροῦ ἀρτάβαι) γ
⌐ κρ(ιθῇ) (ἄρουραι) d η̄ ῑο ξο̄ ἀνὰ (ἀρτάβας) ζ

3 σὺν ρ (γίνονται ἀρτάβαι) γ ⌐ λί(νῳ) (ἄρουραι) d η̄ ῑο ξο̄ ἀνὰ
στ[ίπ]π(ου) δέσμ(ας) ιδ σὺν κ δέσμ(αι) ς ⌐ η̄

4 (γίνονται) σίτ(ου) (πυροῦ ἀρτάβαι) ι ℊ κρ(ιθῆς)
(ἀρτάβαι) ιβ d λί(νου) δέσμ(αι) ς τιμ(ὴ)
χόρ(του) νο(μίσματα) α η̄

5 Ἡλίας Μαρίας ἀπὸ τοῦ αὐ(τοῦ) ἐποικ(ίου) τελ(εῖ) καὶ ἃ ὑπὲρ
ὧν ἐγεώργ(ει) ἀπὸ τοῦ προκ(ειμένου) ἐδάφ(ους)
Ναμ[ ]

6 ἀπὸ (ἀρουρῶν) κ...(ἄρουραι) α ℊ (πυρῷ) (ἄρουραι) ⌐ ῑο
ἀνὰ (πυροῦ ἀρτάβας) ζ σὺν ρ (γίνονται πυροῦ ἀρτάβαι) δ ⌐ χο(ίνικες) δ κρ(ιθῇ) (ἄρουραι) ⌐ ιο

7 ἀνὰ κρ(ιθῆς)(ἀρτάβας) ζ σὺν ρ (γίνονται ἀρτάβαι) δ ⌐
χο(ίνικες) δ λί(νῳ) (ἄρουραι) ⌐ ιο ἀνὰ στίππ(ον)
δέσμ(ας) ιδ σὺ[ν κ]

8 δέσ(μαι) [η d (?)] καὶ ἀπὸ ἐδάφ(ους) Μελανθί(ου) ἀπ'
(ἀρουρῶν) κβ η̄ (ἄρουραι) α ⌐ ὧν λί(νῳ) (ἄρουραι)
ℊ [ἀνὰ]

9 στίππ(ου) δέσμ(ας) [ιζ σὺ]ν κ δέσμ(αι) ιγ ⌐ χόρ(του)
προβ(ατικοῦ) (ἄρουραι) ℊ ἀνὰ (πυροῦ ἀρτάβας) β
σὺν ρ (ἀρτάβαι) [...]

10 καὶ ἀπ' ἐδάφ(ους) Δε..αμεχωτου ἀπ' (ἀρουρῶν) δ (ἄρουραι)
α d ῑο λο̄ ὧν (πυρῷ ἄρουραι) d η̄ ῑο λο̄ ἀνὰ

11 (πυροῦ ἀρτάβας) ζ σὺν ρ (γίνονται πυροῦ ἀρτάβαι) γ ⌐ η̄
κρ(ιθῇ) [(ἄρουραι) d η̄ ῑο λο̄ ἀ]νὰ [(ἀρτάβας) ζ σὺν
ρ (ἀρτάβαι)] γ [⌐ η̄

12 λί(νῳ) (ἄρουραι) d η̄ λο̄ ἀνὰ δέσμ(ας) στίππ(ου) ιδ σὺν κ
δέσμαι στίππ(ου) ...]

Verso

1 .σ. λας Παύλου ἀπὸ τοῦ αὐ(τοῦ) ἐποικ(ίου) τελ(εῖ) ὑπὲρ ὧν
ἐγεώρ(γει) ἐδάφ(ους) Ν.εχαχε

2 ἀπὸ (ἀρουρῶν) κ L ι̅ο̅ (ἄρουραι) β 8/ (πυρῷ ἄρουραι) 8/ [η̅] ἀνὰ
(πυροῦ ἀρτάβας) ζ σὺν ρ (γίνονται ἀρτάβαι) λd
χόρ(τῳ) (ἄρουραι) 8/ η̅
3 ἀνὰ (ἀρτάβας) ζ σὺν ρ (γίνονται ἀρτάβαι) ζd λί(νῳ) (ἄρουραι)
8/ η̅ ἀνὰ στίππ(ου) δέσμ(ας) ιδ σὺν κ
4 δέσμ(αι) ιγ καὶ ἀ̣πὸ ἐδάφ(ους) Μελανθί(ου) ἀπ' ἀρουρῶν) κβ
η̅ (ἄρουραι) α L η̅ ὧν λίν(ῳ) (ἄρουραι) 8/ ι̅ο̅
5 ἀνὰ στίππ(ου) δέσμ(ας) ιζ σὺν κ δέσμ(αι) ιδ Ḷ η̣̅ χόρ(τῳ)
προβ(ατικῷ) (ἄρουραι) 8/ ι̅ο̅ ἀνὰ κρ(ιθῆς) (ἀρτάβας)
β
6 σὺν ρ̣ (ἀρτάβαι) α 8/ χο(ίνικες) β καὶ ἀπὸ ἐδάφ(ους) Πεκυσίου
ἀπ' (ἀρουρῶν) γ (ἄρουρα) α κρ(ιθῇ) ἀνὰ (ἀρτάβας) ζ
7 σὺν ρ (ἀρτάβαι) ζ L χο(ίνικες) η̅ καὶ ἀπὸ ἐδάφ(ους) μεγάλ(ου)
ἀπηλ(ιωτικῆς) σφραγ(ίδος) ἀπ' (ἀρουρῶν) ϛ d
(ἄρουραι) γ η̅
8 ὧν κρ(ιθῇ) (ἄρουρα) α ἀνὰ (ἀρτάβας) ζ σὺν ρ (γίνονται πυροῦ
ἀρτάβαι) ζ L χο(ίνικες) η λί(νῳ) (ἄρουραι) α η̅ ἀνὰ
στίππ(ου) δέσμ(ας) ιδ
9 σ̣ὺ̣ν̣ κ δέσμ(αι) ις Ḷ χόρ(τῳ) (ἄρουρα) α νο( ) L η̅ καὶ ἀπὸ
ἐδάφ(ους) Ζήνωνος ἀπ' (ἀρουρῶν) λζ L
10 (ἄρουραι) ε ὧν κρ(ιθῇ) (ἄρουραι) β 8/ ἀνὰ (ἀρτάβας) ϛ σὺν
ρ (ἀρτάβαι) ιη χο(ίνικες) ϛ λί(νῳ) (ἄρουραι) β d
ἀνὰ στίππ(ου)
11 [δ]έσμ(ας) ιβ[σὺ]ν̣ κ̣ δέσμ(αι) κζ ḍ κ̣α̣ὶ̣ ἀ̣π̣ὸ̣ γεωρ(γοῦ)
[Ἀπ]ολλωνίου ἀ̣π̣ὸ̣ (ἀ̣ρ̣ο̣υ̣ρ̣ῶ̣ν̣) η̅ . . . .
Traces of another line.

"From 29 ar. 1 13/16 ar. in grass at 5/8 solidi per ar. Total 1 1/8 solidi. In the estate of Dep(') from *x* ar. 1 55/64 ar. of which 61/64 ar. in wheat taxed at 7 art. of wheat with supplement of 1% yield 3½ art. of wheat. Also 61/64 ar. in barley taxed at 7 art. of barley with supplement of 1% yield 3½ art. of barley. Also 61/64 ar. in flax taxed at the rate of 14 bundles of flax with supplement of 5% yield 6 5/8 bundles. Total tax paid by *X* 10¾ art. wheat, 12¼ art. barley, 6 bundles of flax, 1 1/8 solidi for hay.

Helias Marias living in the same hamlet also is taxed for the land cultivated by him in the aforesaid estate of Nam( ): from 20-ar. 1¾ ar. are subject to tax of which 9/16 ar. in wheat at 7 art. with supplement of 1% yield 4½ art. 4 choenices; 9/16 ar. in barley at the same rate yield 4½ art. barley and 4 choenices; 9/16 ar. in flax at the rate of 14 bundles with supplement of 5% yield (8¼?) bundles. Also cultivated in the estate of Melanthius 22 1/8 ar. of which 1½ ar. are taxed as follows: ¾ ar. in flax at 17 bundles per ar. with supplement of 5% yielding 13½ bundles; ¾ ar. in hay for fodder at 2 art. of wheat per ar. with supplement of 1% yielding X art. of wheat. Also from 4 ar. in the estate of De . . amechotus $11\frac{1}{32}$ ar. are taxed as follows: $15\frac{5}{32}$ ar. in wheat at 7 art. with supplement of 1% yielding $3\frac{5}{8}$ art.; $15\frac{5}{32}$ ar. in barley at 7 art. with supplement of 1% yielding $3\frac{5}{8}$ art. of barley; $13\frac{3}{32}$ ar. in flax at 14 bundles with supplement of 5% yielding 6(?) bundles of flax.

X son of Paulus living in the same hamlet pays taxes for the $20\frac{7}{12}$ ar. cultivated by him in the estate of N. echache on $2\frac{3}{4}$ ar. as follows: $\frac{7}{8}$ ar. in wheat at 7 art. with supplement of 1% yields $7\frac{1}{4}$ art. of wheat; $\frac{7}{8}$ ar. in grass at 7 art. wheat with supplement of 1% yields $7\frac{1}{4}$ art. wheat; $\frac{7}{8}$ ar. in flax at 14 bundles with supplement of 5% yields 13 bundles. Also from $22\frac{1}{8}$ ar. cultivated in the estate of Melanthius $1\frac{5}{8}$ ar. are taxed as follows: $13\frac{3}{16}$ ar. in flax at 17 bundles with supplement of 5% yield $14\frac{5}{8}$ bundles; $13\frac{3}{16}$ ar. in fodder grass at 2 art. of barley with supplement of 1% yield $1\frac{3}{4}$ art. 2 choenices of barley. Also 3 ar. from the estate of Pekysius of which 1 ar. is taxed at the rate of 7 art. barley with supplement of 1% yielding $7\frac{1}{2}$ art. 8 choinices of barley. Also from the Great Estate in the east sector from a holding of $6\frac{1}{4}$ ar. $3\frac{1}{8}$ ar. are taxed as follows: 1 ar. in barley at the rate of 7 art. wheat with supplement of 1% yielding $7\frac{1}{2}$ art. 8 choenices of wheat; $1\frac{1}{8}$ ar. in flax at the rate of 14 bundles with supplement of 5% yielding $16\frac{1}{2}$ bundles; 1 ar. in hay yielding $\frac{5}{8}$ solidi. Also a holding in the estate of Zenon amounting $33\frac{1}{2}$ ar. of which 5 ar. are taxed as follows: $2\frac{3}{4}$ ar. in barley at 6 art. with supplement of 1% yielding 18 art. 6 choenices; $1\frac{1}{4}$ ar. in flax at 14 bundles with supplement of 5% yielding $27\frac{1}{4}$ bundles. Also from x ar. cultivated by the tenant Apollonius . . . . . . "

Recto 1. The restoration with the article $\tau\tilde{\eta}s$ is uncertain. A break in the papyrus at this point where it was folded shows no indication of any writing on either side of the fold. The tax in money on grass land is 1 solidus later on at Aphrodito (P. Lond. 1433-5). A tax of 1-7 solidi per aroura is found in SPP. X. 144. For $\tau\iota\mu\tilde{\eta}s\ \chi\acute{o}\rho\tau o\upsilon$ but with no indication of rate cf. SPP. X 148.

It is rare for $\dot{\epsilon}\delta\acute{a}\phi\eta$ to have names attached as here. Adjectival names as the estate of Messalina (P. Flor. 40) and public, private, catoecic $\dot{\epsilon}\delta\acute{a}\phi\eta$ are recorded (Preisigke, Wörterbuch, s. v.) are recorded. Whether the names in this document are personal or place name names is uncertain. Melanthius serves both as a personal as well as a place name (cf. P. O. 1285, P. Iand. 63). Similarly Pekusios is a place name ($\tau\acute{o}\pi os\ \Pi\epsilon\kappa\upsilon\sigma\acute{\iota}o\upsilon$) in SPP. X. 45 (Hermopolis). Zenon appears as a personal name, but the *cleros* of Zenon is mentioned in P. Mich. 121, CPR. 10. None of the other forms can be identified either as place or personal names. It is probable that in this document the names represent places. There is no evidence that estates were broken up in this period. Rather the tendency was for their development and growth.

2. Following ρ is the abbreviation for artabas of wheat. Possibly the ligature at the beginning of this line might be called an *iota* signifying 10% but if so it is unlike the usual *iota* which projects high above the line. In P. Iand. 63 (7th cent.) the supplement of 11% is recorded.

4. The scribe omits the fraction of the bundles of hemp (cf. l. 3) in giving the total.

5. The name of the estate may be $N\alpha\mu$( ) or $N\alpha\lambda$( ). This estate apparently was listed in the preceding page.

9. The tax on grass land should be ca. $1\frac{1}{2}$ art. 6 choenices.

11-12. The restoration of these lines is based on the assumption that each taxed area is usually divided into three equal parts but since $11\frac{1}{32}$ ar. cannot be so divided, probably a sixteenth should be deducted from the field in flax. In line 10 it is impossible to read ξo as part of the area. The tax on wheat and barley should be ca. $3\frac{5}{8}$ art., the tax on flax ca. $6\frac{3}{4}$ bundles.

Verso 11. The number of bundles should be $28\frac{1}{4}$, but the horizontal bar preserved immediately above the break in the papyrus seems to indicate the numeral *zeta*. If so, the calculation of the percentage is in error. Apollonius is probably a colonus.

137. OFFICIAL CORRESPONDENCE

GD 7625   9 × 32 cm.   5th or 6th century

The top and right and left margins are preserved, but the bottom is lost. Writer and addressee are unknown, nor do the honorific appellations help much in this period. The letter deals with the collection of arrears of taxation (cf. P. Lips. 64). Vigorous action on the part of the authorities led to full payment within eight days.

Μετὰ τὸ ἐμὲ γράψαι τῆ σῆ ἀρετῆ διὰ Ἡρακλείδου τοῦ Συμμάχου
παρεκλήθη ὁ δεσπότη⟨ς⟩ μου ὁ λαμπρό(τατος)
ἄρχων παρὰ τοῦ περιβλέπτου Ἀνατολίου τοῦ Ἑρμουπολίτου ὥστε
ἐνδοῦναι τοῖς κατεχομένοις
τοῖς ὀφείλουσι παρ[α]στῆσαι τοὺς ἡμῖν τὰ ἐκφόρια χρεωστοῦντες
ἐπαγγειλάμενος
αὐτῶ τῶ λαμπροτάτω ἄρχοντι πέμψαι τὸν βοηθὸν ἅμα Εὐλογίω τῶ
ἀδελφῶ εἰς τοὺς τόπου[ς]
5 [καὶ] ἐπληρώθη [ἡμῖ]ν τὰ χρεωστούμενα ἐκφόρια ἴσω ὀκτὼ
ἡμερῶν [..]ε.υ[.] σ....ν η παρὰ τοῦ
[δ]εσποτ[.............] του ... . τ[ὸ]ν αὐτὸν Εὐλόγιον
ἐκπέμψαι [....]ν παρ [......]σαι ειθ...

"After I had written to Your Excellency by the hand of Heraclides son of Symmachus my master the *clarissimus* magistrate was bidden by the *spectabilis* Anatolius of the Hermopolite nome to give in the names of persons in arrears to those whose duty it is to bring to court delinquent tax-payers, having promised my master the *clarissimus* magistrate, to send his assistant along with his brother Eulogius into the districts. The sums owing were paid in full within eight days ...."

1. For the use of honorary appellatives see Hornickel, Ehren und Rangprädikate, and Preisigke, Wörterbuch, III, Abschnitt 9 (Ehrentitel).

2. ἄρχων. This is probably a state rather than a municipal official. τοῖς κατεχομένοις. Probably τοὺς κατεχομένους should be read.

138. GRAIN RECEIPT

AM 11237   13.2 × 30.3 cm.   6th century

ἐμέτρησεν κληρ(ονόμος) Εὐσεβίου ὀρδιναρίου διὰ Τιμοθέου
ἀπὸ κώμης Πανι( ) ὑπὸ Ἀνηλίου κυβερ(νήτου)

πλοί(ου) Ἰ[ω]άννου Πανερ( ) ὑπὲρ [γενήμα]τος
τεσσερεσκαιδεκάτης ἰνδικ[τίονος]
5 σίτου κανκέλου ἀρτάβας εἴκοσι[— ⸗] κ μώνας
ἄνευ διαπίσματος καὶ προ[σμετ]ρου(μένων)
δι' ἐμοῦ Εὐλογίου σεισειμε[ιώμα]ι.

1. The ordinarius appears in Egypt either as civil or military title in documents of the sixth century. Timotheus appears as ordinarius at Oxyrhynchus (P. O. 942) but is not necessarily to be identified with this Timotheus. On the use in military records see Gilliam, TAPA. LXXI (1941), 127 ff.

2. The name of the village does not appear in Preisigke's Wörterbuch, nor does name Anelius appear in his Namenbuch.

3. The boat seems to belong to John. Names of boats are feminine (Miltner, Pauly-Wissowa, s. v. *Seewesen*). The formula at the end of this line is what we should expect, but the traces of letters actually seem to be . . λιως.

5. The usual formula is μέτρω καγκέλλω. The form μώνας is also found in Kase, Papyrus Roll, instead of μόνας. Its use implies that the extra charges have not been paid.

6. The διαπείσμα is calculated at 11% in P. Iand. 63. This is probably the same as σὺν δεκάταις used in the receipts published by Kase (*loc. cit.*). In general the προσμετρούμενα disappear in the Byzantine period but seemingly certain minor charges were listed under this heading (P. Iand. 63).

139. PETITION AND ACCOUNTS

GD 7550   12 × 16.7 cm.   6th century

The *recto* contains a fragmentary account of some legal proceedings in which 50 pounds of gold were involved. The document is too fragmentary to determine the content, but it gives the date in the reign of Flavius Anastasius (491-512). The *verso* was used at some later time for accounts which are also fragmentary. In the second column payments are made to individuals, soldiers and officials. In the first column it is probable that payments are made to similar groups but the names are lost. In l. 6 the dative is clear, but in l. 2 the form διέγ(ραψε) might imply that the sum was paid as a tax and the entry in l. 9 may be either the sum of tax forwarded or the profit of the owner of the estate to whom this sum was sent. The sums paid out in this column are too large for wages. In P. O. 2045 (A. D. 612) the monthly wage is given as a third of a solidus. The number of solidi in this column is followed by π without any indication of abbreviation but which in accounts always indicates the number of κεράτια deducted from the solidi. The number of carats is regularly a multiple of the number of *nomismata* (cf. P. Baden 94).

Recto

. . . .

τάξει δ· . . . . εσιμον ἢ τοῦ[

τῶν ἑτέρων τοῦ χρ(υσοῦ) λί(τραι) ν κατὰ τὴν[

ἐν ᾧ μ. οὐ μελέτη ἐκθέσθαι γραμμ[

5   προστεταγμένους τὰς ἐπαγωγίμας[

ἐν τῷ ἡγεμονικῷ δικαστηρίῳ[

πάντα νικῶ[ντος] θεοῦ καὶ δεσπότου ἡμῶν[

Φλ(αουίου) Ἀναστασίου τοῦ αἰωνίου Αὐγούστου α[ὐτοκράτορος]

]τοῦ εἰρημένου ἐνδοξοτάτου[

10   ἀ]κολουθῶς ὑποθε[

Verso

Col. 1

	{ νο(μίσματα)	ι	π	λ }
διέγρ(αψε)	νο( )	κ	π	ξ
	{ νο( )	λ	π	[.] }
	νο( )	ι	π	λ
5	{ νο( )	λ	π	ϙ}
αριω	νο( )	ε	π	ιε
{ τῆς αὐτῆς Παλ( )	νο( )	κε	π	οε }
ὑπὲρ τοῦ (ἔτους) η				
τοῦ ὅλου . . . σταλ(έντος)	νο( )	μ	π	ρκ
10	νο( )	ι	π	με
. . . . .	νο( )	κε	πα(ρα)	κε

Col. 2

Ἀραβικῆ[

τοῖς ἐπ. . .[

{ τοῖς στρατι(ώταις) }

Παλλαδίω[

5   Θεοφίλω[

{ τοῖς ξενοῖ[ς   }

    (γίνεται) νο(μίσματα) ρκ ..

    ὑπὲρ τοῦ Ἴστρ(ου)

    Πασίων Ἰωά[ννου

10   ὑπ(ὲρ) Μηνύθεως[

{ τοῖς ξένοις στρ[ατιώταις   }

    τοῖς αὐγουστάλ(οις)

    τῷ βοηθ(ῷ) τῆς Α[

{   .....κ...ικ...   }

140. Tax Assessment

GD 7652   6th or 7th century

These two leaves form part of a record of payments. Page I (15.5 × 17.5 cm.) is broken at top and bottom but the entries on the *recto* start some distance below the top of the fragment as at present preserved. Page II (19.5 × 17.5 cm.) is broken at the top. The total given at the bottom of col. 1 is apparently much greater than the payments of this column, and probably represents the total of a single day's receipts some of which were recorded on preceding pages. The total in col. 2 is much higher and evidently some of the contributors in the lost portion paid in solidi. In line 16 it is possible that the clerk carried over the total of col. 1, and the addition in l. 17 is slightly incorrect. There is no evidence of totals at the bottom of the columns on the *verso* and the presumption is that these represent incomplete daily (or monthly) returns.

Payments vary from a fourth of a *keration* to 33 solidi. Most of the payments are small and the variation in amount seems to imply an assessment based on property (cf. P. Russ. Georg. IV. 18, P. Lond. 1028, 1421, P. Cairo 67142).

Many of the names are new and in some cases the division between name and patronymic is mere guess work. Sometimes initial *iota* is indicated by a curved line above the letter but the scribe is not always consistent in this practice. In a few cases a superimposed letter indicates an abbreviation. The sign for *keratia* is a slanting bar.

Page I *recto,* Col. 1

(Space for two lines (2 cm.) blank at top)

δ(ιὰ) Λε......   / [ ]
δ(ιὰ) Αβρ.......   / ιϛ └

(Space for two entries apparently blank. Surface much worn.)

[δ(ιὰ) ....]αα[.....]   / ιγ
δ(ιὰ) Σ..χι..αμο..   / δ
5 δ(ιὰ) Μηνο Χαρησίο(ν)   / α d
δ(ιὰ) Κυριακο(ῦ) Ἐλάου   / ιϛ
δ(ιὰ) Ἰσακίο(ν) Σκατ( )   / .
δ(ιὰ) τ(οῦ) Τεκνω( ) Νουνε   / δ
δ(ιὰ) Καλαπησίο(ν) ἄπα Λιτ( )   / α └
10 δ(ιὰ) Πακτ Συρι   / δ
[δ(ιὰ) ....   ]
δ(ιὰ) Κολλούθο(ν) Ταπι.   / κ └
δ(ιὰ) Ἰωάννο(ν) Νον ..   νο( ) α
δ(ιὰ) Ἀζαρίας Λο( )   / δ

Page I *recto,* Col. 2

(Space of 6 cm. at top is without entries)

δ(ιὰ) Κακει...   / [ ]
δ(ιὰ) Χράνιος Κουφο[ ]   / [ ]
δ(ιὰ) Ψουπάνο(ν) Παμφ( )   / [ ]
δ(ιὰ) Ἰακώβο(ν) Παμφ( )   / └
5 δ(ιὰ) Ἀπαδίο(ν) Ταλο( )   / └ d
δ(ιὰ) Παχυμίο(ν)   / δ └ d
δ(ιὰ) Πατιλ( ) Ἰουθιο..   / . d
δ(ιὰ) [..] .. [....]   ]
[δ(ιὰ) ..]πω..δ..κ..   / └ d
10 δ(ιὰ) ..ελουτα( ) Τσελει   / κ └ d
δ(ιὰ) Ἰωάννο(ν) Φρα..ε( )   / ϛ d
δ(ιὰ) τοῦ Σασνῶ γναφ(εύς)   νο( ) α / ιβ

Page I *verso,* Col. 1

[δ(ιὰ) . . .]ωμηις   / . .
[δ(ιὰ) . . .]αρος Καφοητ( )   / γ└
 δ(ιὰ) Βαρσάκ   / α
 δ(ιὰ) Ἀνανίας Χυρτιπε   / ις
5 δ(ιὰ) Ἀνανίας Ψάχ   / α└ d
 δ(ιὰ) Μῆνος Παάμ   / └
[δ(ιὰ) . . . Χ]υρτιπε   / α .
 δ(ιὰ) το(ῦ) Ἀκ[   ]   / α└
 δ(ιὰ) Ῥωβ[/]
10 δ(ιὰ) Λεωμαι Εἰσοπολιτ( )   / ια [ ]
 δ(ιὰ) Ἀβραάμ   / ζ└
 δ(ιὰ) το(ῦ) Λεπτο Κιλ( )   νο( ) δ   / └
 δ(ιὰ) Κα[. . .]και   / ις└
 δ(ιὰ) Ζαχαρία Πωη( )   / α└
15 δ(ιὰ) Ἀαλιλ( ) Ἀπιοικ   / ε└ d
 δ(ιὰ) Πατυρμ( ) Ἐλιουζγ( )   / κ└ d
 δ(ιὰ) Μην Κλαμησια   / α d
 δ(ιὰ) Σῖμος   / ια
 δ(ιὰ) Κ[. . . .] Ἐλιουζγ( )   [ ]
20 δ(ιὰ) Μην . Κανα( )   / ε└ d
 δ(ιὰ) Πααφ [. . .]ψ   / ι [. .]
 δ(ιὰ) Ἰσὰκ Σκατ( )   / α
 δ(ιὰ) Σεν( ) Σκατ( )   / ς
 δ(ιὰ) το(ῦ) Νοκνε   / ς

Page I *verso,* Col. 2

 δ(ιὰ) Γ . . μολ   / . .
 δ(ιὰ) ἄπα Δι( ) Σαι   / . .
 δ(ιὰ) Πάπα Κικι   / ι [ ]
 δ(ιὰ) Ἀρυο( ) Σαι   / κα d
5 δ(ιὰ) Σάμψων Ἰσάκ   / α└
 δ(ιὰ) Κ[. . .]ν Σαι   / κ└
 δ(ιὰ) [. . .]κνεαμι   / κδ

δ(ιὰ)	[. . .]σιω[. .]αλι	νο( ) α	/ κγ
δ(ιὰ)	Πασκ Σ[. . .]		/ ς d
10 δ(ιὰ)	Πεσον Προσοπ( )	νο( ) λγ	/ ιθ
δ(ιὰ)	Ἀνθειλι Νοως		/ ια
δ(ιὰ)	[. . . .]ρ Παθοος	νο( ) α	/ γ
δ(ιὰ)	Βενθ( ) Ταβιθα		/ θ └
δ(ιὰ)	ἄπα Κυρι γναφ(εύς)		/ α
15 δ(ιὰ)	Κυριακός		/ α d
δ(ιὰ)	Ἐπιφ Πιε( )	νο( ) α	/ ις
δ(ιὰ)	Ζαχαρία . Παυλ( )	νο( ) α	/ ιθ └
[δ(ιὰ)	. . .]κειωτ( )		[ ]
δ(ιὰ)	Ἰσὰκ Πλητ( )		/ α [ ]
20 δ(ιὰ)	Ἀνανία[ς] Κοφοκ		/ ς
δ(ιὰ)	Ἰωά(ννου) Παμφίλια		/ ιδ d
δ(ιὰ)	Ἰακῶβ ἀδελφοῦ		/ ιδ

Page II *recto,* Col. 1

δ(ιὰ)	Ἰακώβο(υ) Δουλία		/ ια
δ(ιὰ)	Ἰακώβο(υ) Καθωτα		/ ιγ
δ(ιὰ)	Ἐπιφανίου Δαρ . α		/ ις └
δ(ιὰ)	Χαταπε		/ α η
5 δ(ιὰ)	Σεπακυρο(υ) Ἀνατολι		/ κδ
δ(ιὰ)	Πιυτσοι Καλχ[. .]		/ α └
δ(ιὰ)	Ἀνδρθο(υ) Ραπίο(υ)		/ κ └ η
δ(ιὰ)	Δανιηλίο(υ) Πενγαμ		/ Ⴢ d
δ(ιὰ)	Σουαι( ) Ταναιε		/ κ └ η
10 δ(ιὰ)	Καμσουάκ		/ γ └
δ(ιὰ)	Σάμψων Καρπα		/ γ └
δ(ιὰ)	Κωσταντίνο(υ)	νο( ) β	/ α
δ(ιὰ)	Καμητ Ἀπία		/ ς
δ(ιὰ)	Ἰσακίο(υ) Λάο(υ) Νοως		/ κ └
15 δ(ιὰ)	τ(οῦ) Τεκτ . . νο		/ γ
δ(ιὰ)	τ(οῦ) Καμήο(υ) Λιτ( )		/ θ └ d
δ(ιὰ)	ἄπα Δίο(υ) Σαι( )		/ κ
δ(ιὰ)	Πάπας Κικι		/ [‥]
δ(ιὰ)	Σάμψων		/ [‥]
20	νο( ) ιζ / θ		

Page II *recto,* Col. 2

δ(ιὰ) Ἀναστασίο							/ ι
δ(ιὰ) Καμῆς Ἀρρῆς					νο( ) δ	/ κ
δ(ιὰ) Πάπας Θίο(υ) ἀπ(ὸ) τ(ῆς) ἐκκ(λησίας)				/ α d
δ(ιὰ) Μυσαίο(υ) ἀπ(ὸ) Φολ( )			νο( ) .	/ ι
5 δ(ιὰ) ἄπ|α] Κάρο(υ) Σαμ( )						/ ⌞
δ(ιὰ) Κεαρσίο(υ) Ἐνκιτο( )			νο( ) δ	/ ι d
δ(ιὰ) Σάσνω υἱοῦ							/ ιγ d
δ(ιὰ) Λεοντί(υ) Πορτ( )						/ κ d
δ(ιὰ) Ἰσακίο(υ) Π..ιτ( )						/ . ⌞
10 δ(ιὰ) τ(οῦ) Σιτάνο(υ) φύλακ(ος)			νο( ) α
δ(ιὰ) τ(οῦ) Χε.οικμαλ( ) τῆ(ς) ἐκκ(λησίας)				/ κγ d
δ(ιὰ) Ἰωάννο(υ) Δανηλίο(υ)						/ ιγ d
δ(ιὰ) Σι.ε.νο......						/ γ ⌞
δ(ιὰ) ...							(blank)
15				νο( ) κη / κα

(Three lines space with no entries)

				νο( ) ι ...

(Two lines space with no entries)

				νο( ) μς ς

Page II *verso,* Col. 1

δ(ιὰ) Αμα..κι( )							/ . ⌞
δ(ιὰ) Πακτ( ) Αρ							/ δ
δ(ιὰ) Θεοδοσίο(υ) Ἰωά(ννου)			νο( ) α	/ ιβ ⌞
δ(ιὰ) Κολλοθ( ) Ταπιο( )						/ ς ⌞ d
5 δ(ιὰ) Λεκα( ) Ταματι( )						/ β ⌞
δ(ιὰ) Ἰω[...]καδ( )						α ⌞
δ(ιὰ) Ἀζαρίας							/ α
δ(ιὰ) Μηνο Ἀάνιρε( )						/ β ⌞
δ(ιὰ) Κενοραι Γεβοσε						/ α ⌞
10 δ(ιὰ) Ἰακῶβ Ἀλλιε( )						/ ιγ ⌞
δ(ιὰ) Ἰακῶβ Καθυτι						/ γ

δ(ιὰ) Ἐπιφαλιμι⟨ο⟩ς   / ις └
         Χαταπε   / ιβ
δ(ιὰ) Πακυρι( )   κ [ ]
15 δ(ιὰ) Ạιγγ. . καμαιε   / α └
[δ(ιὰ) . . . .]καραπου   [ ]
δ(ιὰ) Δανιὴλ Πανβα   / ι d
δ(ιὰ) Συ( ) Σαι γναφ(εύς)   / ι
δ(ιὰ) Καμσο( ) Ακ( )   / └
20 δ(ιὰ) Σάμψων Καρτ( )   / γ └

The remainder of column is blank.

Page II *verso*, Col. 2

δ(ιὰ) Παχιρω   / ια
δ(ιὰ) Παχουμπαι   / α └ d
δ(ιὰ) Παλπιθ( ) Ἀπαιδ( )   / α └
δ(ιὰ) Πλετρο( ) Ἀπτερο   / κ └
5 δ(ιὰ) Η[. . . .]θ   / δ
δ(ιὰ) Π[ά]σκος Κοιακ   / ζ └ d
δ(ιὰ) Πεκμ Παγλεαετ( )   / κ └ d
δ(ιὰ) Ἰωάν[νου] Παπθ( )   / δ └ d
δ(ιὰ) Σασνᾶ γναφ(εύς)   νο( ) δ   / ιβ
10 δ(ιὰ) Ἀναστασι   / ιδ
δ(ιὰ) Καράκ   / κα
δ(ιὰ) Παπθ( ) ἀπὸ τῆ(ς) ἐκκ(λησίας)   / ε d
δ(ιὰ) Μοσαιο( ) Παοφιλ( )   νο( ) β   / κα └
δ(ιὰ) Ωσιεπιφ   / └
15 δ(ιὰ) Κ[. . . .]κμο[. .]αμ   / └
δ(ιὰ) Ἰ[σά]κ Το[. .]   νο( ) α   / κα
δ(ιὰ) Σαννω Σι( )   / γ d
δ(ιὰ) Λεοντι[ου]. ρ   / κα
δ(ιὰ) Ἰσάκ Που( )   / α └
20 δ(ιὰ) Σιγνο φύλαξ   νο( ) α
δ(ιὰ) Α[. .]μασχο   / δ └
διὰ   Καπελφι   / ιγ d
δ(ιὰ) Ἰωά(ννου) Δανιὴλ   / ιγ d
δ(ιὰ) Ἰσμεα. Ζαλλ( )   / ς └

PRIVATE DOCUMENTS

A. LOANS

141. RECEIPT FOR LOAN

AM 11228 A   20 × 15 cm.   A. D. 23

This receipt is of interest because of the spelling. The same scribe wrote no. 142 where similar peculiarities are found. The mention of the record office in the middle toparchy probably indicates that the document comes from Oxyrhynchus.

Τάσευς Πεγύσιος μετὰ γυρίου τοῦ πατρὸς Πεγύσιος τοῦ Πεγύσιος ἀπέχω τὰς τοῦ ἀργυρίου δραχμὰς τριακοσίας καὶ τοὺς τούτους δόκους καὶ οὐθὲν ἐνκαλῶ καθότι πρόκειται, Διονύσιος Ἀσ-
κληπιάδου ἔγραψα ὑπὲρ αὐτῶν διὰ τὸ μὴ εἰτέναι αὐ[τ]οὺς
5 γράμματα

(2nd hand) ἔτους δεκάτου [Τ]ιβερίου Καίσαρος Σεβαστοῦ
        Μεχειρ κέ
        δι' Ἀλεξάνδρου τοῦ πρὸς τῶι γραφίωι μέσης το-
        παρχίας
    Verso
        ἀποχ(ρεία) Τασευτος πρὸς Διον[ ]

1. Πεγύσιος l. Πεκύσιος : γυρίου l. κυρίου
2. τούτους l. τούτων
3. δόκους l. τόκους
4. εἰτέναι l. εἰδέναι

"I, Taseus daughter of Pekysis with my guardian who is my father Pekysis son of Pekysis, acknowledge the receipt of 300 silver dr. and the interest thereon, and I have no further claim as above. I, Dionysius son of Asclepiades, wrote on their behalf as they are ignorant of letters.

The 10th year of Tiberius Caesar Augustus. Mechir 25. Recorded by Alexander in charge of the record office of the middle toparchy."

For the interchange of gutturals, cf. Mayser, Grammatik, I, 169; for interchange of dentals, *ibid.* 175.

142. LOAN OF MONEY

AM 11226 C   9.5 × 10.5 cm.   ca. 23 A. D.

Peculiarities of hand and spelling place this document as a contemporary of no. 141.

```
     .τα [. .] . .          [οὐ-]
     λῆ γόνατι ἀριστερῶ ἔχειν
     παρὰ ⟨αὐτῆς⟩ τὸν ὁμολογοῦντα Νεῖ-
     λον δειὰ χειρὸς χρῆσιν κεφα-
  5  λαίου ἀργυρίου δραχμὰς διακο-
     σίας εἴκοσι τέσσαρος τόγου
     δραχμιαίου ἑκάστη μνᾶ κα-
     τὰ μῆνα καὶ πάνακον αὐτ-
     ὸν ἀποτώσιν τῇ Κολλαῦθι
 10  τό δε κεφάλαιον καὶ τοὺς τό-
     γους μηνὶ Παῦνι τοῦ ἐνεστώ-
     τος ἔτους τῆς πράξεως οὔ-
     σης τῇ Κολλαῦθι ἔκ ˋτέˊ τοῦ Νείλου καὶ
     ἐκ τῶν ὑπαρχόντων αὐτῶ πάν-
 15  των (2nd hand) παχατωσαντο( ) καθαιυμαιηρακισιοθ( )
```

4. δειὰ l. διὰ
6. τέσσαρος l. τέσσαρες; τόγου l. τόκου, cf. also l. 10
8. πάνακον l. ἐπάναγκον
9. ἀποτώσιν l. ἀποδώσειν
10. δε l. τε

"(Agreement between Kollauthis and Nilus who is aged x years and has a) scar on his left knee. The latter acknowledges that he has from her the loan of 224 dr. in silver with interest at a drachma per mina per month and that of necessity he will pay Kollauthis both principal and interest in Payni of the current year. Kollauthis has the right of exaction from Nilus and from all his property."

3. The document is meaningless without the insertion of αὐτῆς. Cf. BGU. 290. ἔχειν παρ' αὐτοῦ τὸν ὁμολογοῦντα κτλ.

15. The cursive script has so far defied attempts at decipherment. Normally the formula of exaction should end καὶ ἐκ τῶν αὐτῷ ὑπαρχόντων πάντων καθάπερ ἐκ δίκης but this is not the case here. There is no evidence that the signatures of either party were affixed nor is the formula on behalf of illiterates used.

143. PAYMENT OF DEBT

GD 7601 R   20 × 8 cm.   3rd century

Itibus Decem[bribus]
nomine in solutum ex pretio   X $\overline{xxx}$
mercium Julio Agathemero
numeravit Julio Agathaio

Itibus for *Idibus.*

One of these persons is probably to be construed as the subject of the verb *numeravit*, and the scribe may have been influenced by the dative form in l. 3 to write Julius Agathaeus incorrectly in the same case. The line above the denarii implies that the sum is 30,000, and probably the document should be dated in the inflationary period of the early 4th century, though the hand seems to be earlier (Thompson, Palaeography, Plate on p. 317).

144. LOAN OF MONEY

AM 8940   12 × 18.5 cm.   Early 3rd century

This papyrus is badly worm-eaten and has lost considerable portions on both sides. Originally folded in narrow strips about 2 cm. wide, one, or perhaps two, of these have disappeared on the left, and on the right hand side only a small portion at the bottom remains of the outer strip. The restorations offered for the first six lines are indications of the probable length of lines more than anything else.

This antichretic loan where the right of *habitatio* is given in place of interest has other prototypes, though complete documents are few (See Economic Survey of Roman Egypt 262). However the records of the grapheion at Tebtynis for A. D. 45-47 (P. Mich. 123R) show that 35 such transactions were entered during a period of 16 months. For a discussion of this type of transaction see P. Hamb. 30 and bibliography there cited.

Usually the rate of interest is specified but in this case there is no room for the usual formula. In most loans the borrower agrees to repay his loan in Payni or Epiph, but this contract seems to be dated about this time and the right of habitatio begins in Epiph. The restoration of lines 11, 14 is as yet unsolved. In the former there was probably a description of the house; in the latter some such phrasing as this ' nor is it permitted Aurelius Diogenes to alienate etc.' may be restored. In l. 19 the subjunctive ποιήσηται seems to have been an error for the future indicative. For παράθεσις see the discussion by Flore, Aegyptus VIII (1927), 67 ff. The library or record office of Apollinarius is new but the reading is none too certain.

The principals of this contract also appear in the records of the Temple of Jupiter Capitolinus at Ptolemais (BGU. 362) which belongs in approximately the same period.

῎Ετους τρ]ίτου [Αὐ]τοκρ[άτορος
Εὐσεβοῦς Ε]ὐτυχο|ῦς Σεβαστοῦ Παῦνι, ἐν Πτολεμάιδι
Εὐεργέ]τιδι τοῦ Ἀρσιν[οίτου νομοῦ. Ὁμολογεῖ Αὐρήλιος
Διογένης ὡς] ἐτῶν ἑ[βδομήκοντα?.]ουλ[ὴ . . . .
5 . . . .] Αὐρηλίῳ Σερήν[ῳ τῷ καὶ] Ἰσι[δώρῳ Ὀλύμπου . . .
. . . . . .ὡς ἐτ]ῶν πεντήκοντα [. . . . ἔχειν παρὰ Αὐρηλίου
Σερήνου τοῦ κ(αὶ) Ἰσιδώρο]υ τοῦ Ὀλύμπου ἐκ [τοῦ α]ὐτοῦ [ἀμφόδου
χρῆσιν ἀργυρίου κεφ]αλαίου δραχμὰς διακοσίας ἐπὶ [τῇ] ἐν[οικήσει
. . . . . . .τοῦ ὑπάρχ]οντος αὐτοῦ περὶ κώμην Φιλαδελφε[ίαν . . . . . .
10 τοῦ αὐτοῦ] Ἀρσινοίτου νο[μοῦ] ἥμισον μέρος οἰκ[ίας . . . .
. . . .].. μινα . . . . . .ροτον πρὸς τὸν [. . . . .
ἀπὸ τοῦ εἰσι]όντος μηνὸ[ς Ἐπ]εὶφ τοῦ ἐνεστῶ[τος ἔτους . . . .
εἰ δὲ μὴ ἀ]πόδοτόν ἐστι τὸ προκείμενον κ[εφάλαιον . . . .
. . . .]. . .ουσι . . . . σερητιου δι..απ[. . . . .
15 κυριεύει]ν τοῦ προκει[μένου] ἡμίσους μέρο[υς οἰκίας . . . .
. . . .]αροντων πα. . . . . ἀλλοτριῶσαι[. . . . .
ἄνευ χρη]ματισμοῦ ἄχρις ἂν ἀποδῇ τὸ προκ[είμενον . . . .
κεφάλαιο]ν καὶ ὅπαν βούληται ἐκ τοῦ πρ[οειρημένου μηνὸς
Ἐπεὶφ . . . .]παράθεσιν ποιήσηται καὶ ..[. . . . .
20 . . . .]ον βιβλιοθήκης Ἀπολλιναρίου [. . . . . .της δὲ
πράξεως γε]νομένης Αὐρηλίῳ Σερήνῳ τῷ [καὶ Ἰσιδώρῳ παρὰ
Αὐρηλίου] Διογένους καὶ ἐκ τοῦ ἡμίσου μέρους οἰκίας [καὶ] ἐκ

τῶν ὑπαρ]χόντων αὐτῶ πάντων καθάπερ ἐκ δίκης
Ὁμολογεῖ Αὐρή]λιος Διογένης οὐετρανὸς ἐγ. . . .ανου
25 δανεῖσθαι δρα]χμὰς διακοσίας ἐπὶ τῆ ἐνοικήσι ἀντὶ
τῶν τόκω]ν τοῦ προκειμένου κεφαλαίου ὡς πρόκειται.

"In the third year of the emperor .... Pauni . at Ptolemais Euergetis in the
Arsinoite nome. Aurelius Diogenes, aged about 70, and marked with a scar, acknowledges to Aurelius Serenus also called Isidorus son of Olympus that he has received
from him a loan of 200 silver dr. and in lieu of interest Serenus has the right to inhabit
the half part of a house belonging to Diogenes near the village of Philadelphia ......
from the coming month Epiph of the current year. If the aforesaid sum is not paid
back (within a specified time) Serenus will have the ownership of the aforesaid half
portion of the house ..... nor shall Diogenes alienate this property until he pays back
the aforesaid loan. Whenever he wishes Serenus may register this contract in the
record-office of Apollinarius(?). Aurelius Serenus has the right of exaction from
Aurelius Diogenes in person and from the half part of the house and from all his
possessions as if legal decision had been given.
Aurelius Diogenes, veteran .... acknowledges that he has borrowed 200 dr. with the
right of habitatio in lieu of interest on the aforesaid principal as stated above."

145. LOAN

GD 7528   10.5 × 12.5 cm.   6th century

Aurelius George, stable-master, and his wife agree to repay a loan
of four solidi in the month Pharmouthi when they receive advance
payments on their salary for the fifteenth indiction.

[ἅπερ ἀκίνδυνα]
ὄντα ἀπὸ παντὸς κινδύνου ὁμολογοῦμεν
διδόναι τῆ σῆ θαυμασιότητι ἐν τῶ Φαρμοῦθι
μηνὶ τῆς παρούσης τεσσαρασκαιδεκάτης
5 ἰνδικτίονος ἠνίκα δεχόμεθα
ἀραβῶνας τῶν ἡμῶν μισθῶν τῆς
πέντε καὶ δεκάτης ἐπινεμήσεως ἀνυπερ-
θέτως κινδύνω τῶν ἡμῖν ὑπαρχόντων
ὑποκειμένων κύριον τὸ γραμματῖον
10 ἁπλοῦν γραφέν καὶ ἐπερρ(ωτηθέντες) ὡμολογήσαμεν
† Αὐρήλιος Γεώργιος ἀρχισταβλίτης υἱὸς
Βίκτωρος καὶ ἡ τούτου γαμετὴ Εὐφημία
θυγατὴρ Ἀγοῦπ οἱ προγεγραμμένοι πεποιήμεθα

τοῦτο τὸ γραμμ(ατῖον) τῶν τεσσάρων νομισμ(άτων) ὡς πρό-
κ(ειται)

15 Ἰωάννης υἱὸς τοῦ μακαρίου Ἰσὰκ ἀξιωθεὶ(ς) ἔγραψα
ὑπὲρ αὐτῶν γράμματ[α μὴ εἰδότων]

Initial iota and upsilon are marked with diaeresis throughout.

"(This sum) we agree to pay to your excellency in Pharmouthi of the present 14th
indiction when we receive earnest-money of our pay for the 15th indiction. This we do
without delay pledging the property which belongs to us. This contract is valid and is
in one copy. On being questioned we acknowledged the contract. Aurelius Georgius,
stablemaster, and his wife Euphemia, daughter of Anoup have made this contract
for four pieces of money (solidi) as above. John, son of the blessed Isaac, wrote on
their behalf as they are unlettered."

3. θαυμασιότης. This appellative appears first ca. 361, Hornickel, *op. cit.*

6. ἀραβῶνας. This offers an interesting sidelight on government employment if earnest-
money was given in advance to retain the services of employees. If this is the
case, one must infer that labor was difficult to secure or else George was
unusually efficient. Yet it appears from the statement of the scribe that he was
unlettered in spite of the responsibility of his post.

11. ἀρχισταβλίτης. This title first appears in 706/7 (P. Lond. 1433), but undoubtedly
existed earlier as σταβλίτης appears in 550 (P. O. 140). For the postal service
see Wilcken, Grundzüge 372 ff.; Seeck, *Cursus Publicus,* PWRE. IV 1846 ff.

B. LEASES AND SALES

146. ·LEASE OF PUBLIC LAND

AM 11230   8 × 15 cm.   Tebtynis A. D. 36

Six years later the same Marsisuchus subleased five arouras of public
land from Hatres, son of Phanes, near the great road in the southern
sector (P. Mich. 121 R. II. vi). In the present lease the five ar. are
also called public land, but are designated as lying in the newly planted
section. In both cases the lessor is styled ' Persian of the epigone,'
receiving the rental in advance (προδοματικὴ μίσθωσις). The lessor
thus has the status of a debtor and forfeits any right of asylum in case
of prosecution by the creditor (Tait, Archiv, VII (1924), 175-182;
von Woess, Asylwesen, 60-74; Pringsheim, Zeitschr. der Savigny-
Stiftung, Röm. Abt. XLIV (1924), 396-456; Schönbauer, *ibid.* XLIX
(1929), 359-367).

Ἔτους δευτέρου καὶ εἰκοστοῦ Τιβ[ερίου Καίσαρος]
Σεβαστοῦ μηνὸς Δαισίου ἕκτη [καὶ εἰκοστὴ(?) ἐν Τε-]
βτύνει τῆς Πολέμωνος μερίδος [τοῦ Ἀρσινοΐτου]
νομοῦ ἐμίσθωσεν Μαρεψῆ[μις ὅς κ(αὶ) (?)   ]
5 Μαρεψήμιος Πέρσης [τῆς ἐπιγονῆς ὡς ἐτῶν]
τεσσαράκοντα πέντε [οὐλὴ   ]
Μαρσισούχωι Μαρεψήμιος ὡς ἐτ[ῶν πεντήκον-]
τα οὐλὴ πήχει δεξιῶι ἐμίσθω[σεν x ἀρούρας]
ἀφ' ὧν καὶ αὐτὸς ὁ Μαρεψῆμις γεω[ργεῖ περὶ Τεβ-]
10 τῦνιν δημοσίων ἐδ[άφων
ἀρουρῶν πέντε ἢ [ὅσαι ἐὰν ὦσιν
ἐπὶ τοῦ νεοφύτου [χωρίου
τοῦ Μαρσισούχου χωρηγοῦντος [ἑαυτῶι τὰ σπέρ-]
ματα εἰς τὸ εἰσιὸν τρίτον καὶ ε[ἰκοστὸν ἔτος]
15 Τιβερίου Καίσαρος Σεβαστοῦ καὶ [ἀπέχει παρὰ]
τοῦ Μαρσισούχου τὸν φόρον π[αράχρημα διὰ χειρὸς
ἐκ προδόματος [καὶ ταύτην τὴν μίσθωσιν]
βα[ι]βαιώσι ὁ Μ[αρεψῆμις πρὸς τὸν Μαρσισοῦχον]
πάσῃ βαιβαιώσι ἀ[πὸ δ]ημοσίων τελεσμάτων
20 καὶ εἰδιωτικῶν καὶ πα[ντὸς εἴδους κτλ.

"The 22nd year of Tiberius Caesar Augustus. Daisius 26. At Tebtynis in the division of Polemon in the Arsinoite nome. Marepsemis also called x son of Marepsemis, Persian of the *epigone*, about 40 years old and marked with a scar on ...... has leased to Marsisuchus son of Marepsemis about 50 years old and marked with a scar on his right thigh *x* arouras from the five ar. or however many there may be of public land near Tebtynis in the New Planting. Marsisuchus is to provide himself with seed for the incoming 23rd year of Tiberius. Marepsemis has received from Marsisuchus the rental forthwith in advance and Marepsemis guarantees this lease to Marsisuchus with every guarantee from all public and private charges .... "

147. LEASE OF LAND

GD 7520   10.5 × 17 cm.   87/88 A. D.

The lease follows the usual form. Lease for one year of a radish-garden, with rent at the rate of two artabae of radish-seed per aroura. Similar leases of radish-gardens are unknown in Roman times (Economic Survey of Roman Egypt, 83 ff.). The crop was raised for its oil, which was worth about half the price of good olive oil (BGU. 14).

ἐμίσθωσεν ['Ιε]ρακίαινα 'Ηρώδου τῶν
ἀπ' 'Οξυρύγ[χ]ων πόλεως μετὰ κυ-
ρ[ίο]υ τοῦ ἑαυτῆς ἀνδρὸς 'Απολλωνίου τοῦ 'Απο[λ]λωνίου Αὐνᾶι ὡς 'Ηρᾶτι
5 'Αρμιύσιος τοῦ Μύλωνος τῶν ἀπὸ Σύ-
ρων κώμης Πέρσῃ τῆς ἐπιγονῆς
εἰς τὸ ἐνεστὸς ἕβδομον ἔτος
Α[ὐ]τοκρά[τορος] Καί[σ]αρος Δομιτιανοῦ
Σεβαστοῦ Γερμανικοῦ ἀπὸ τῶ⟨ν⟩ ὑπαρ-
10 χόντων αὐτῇ περὶ Νέσλα ἐδάφων
τὰς λιμνασθείσας ἀρούρας πάσης
ὥστε ταύτας σπε[ῖ]ραι ῥαφάνῳ ἐκ-
φορίου ἑκάστης ἀρούρης ἐκ γεομε-
τρίας ἐκς [ὀ]ρθογωνίου ἀνὰ ῥαφανο-
15 σπέρμου ἀρτάβας δύο, ἀκίνδυνα
τὰ ἐκφόρ[ι]α παντὸς κινδύνου
τῶν τῆς γῆς δημοσίων ὄντων πρὸ-
ς τὴν 'Ιερακίαινα ἦν καὶ κυριεύειν
τῶν ἐδάφων ἕως τὰ ἐκφόρια κομί-
20 σηται τῆς δὲ μισθώσεως βεβαιω-
μένης ἀποδότω ὁ μεμισ[θ]ώμεν-
ος τῇ 'Ιερακίαινα τὰ ἐκφόρια τῷ Παῦνι μηνὶ τοῦ αὐτοῦ ἔτους ἐφ' ἅλῳ
Νέσλα ῥαφανόσπερμον νέον κα-
25 θαρὸν ἄδολον κεκοσκιναυμένο-
[ν] μέτρῳ τετραχυνεικῷ τῷ τοῦ
[με]μισθωμένου ἁδρῷ ὑπερέχον
[τι τοῦ μ]έτρου Σεράπιδος ταυ-
[. . . . . . .] . νου ἀποτεισάτω αυ
30 [. . . . . . .] . φ. . [. .]ση μεθ' ἡμιολίας

25. l. κεκοσκινευμένο[ν]. This interchange of ευ and αυ is perhaps peculiar to the
Egyptian dialect. Cf. Mayser I. 17. 2 pp. 113 f.
26. l. τετραχοινικῷ
29. l. ἀποτισάτω.

"Hierakiaena daughter of Herodes a citizen of Oxyrhynchus acting with her
guardian who is her husband Apollonius son of Apollonius has leased to Aunas also

called Heras son of Harmiusis son of Mylon from the village of the Syrians, Persian of the *epigone,* for the current 7th year of the emperor Caesar Domitian Augustus Germanicus from the property belonging to her all the flooded land near Nesla to be sown with raphanus at a rental of 2 artabas of raphanus seed per ar. free from all risk. The public taxes on the land shall be paid by Hierakiaena who shall also exercise ownership over the fields until she receives the rental. When the lease is guaranteed the lessee shall pay to Hierakiaena the rental in Payni of the same year at the threshing floor at Nesla in fresh clean sifted unadulterated raphanus seed in the four-choenix measure of the lessee in full measure exceeding the standard of Serapis. (Here follows a clause providing for a penalty of 50% in case the lessee violates the terms of the lease.)"

6.   Πέρση τ. ἐ. See Introduction to no. 146.

27.   ἀδρῷ. Not found elsewhere with measures. Probably implies a well-rounded
       measure. The variety of measures current in Egypt is large and private
       measures are not unknown. The Temple of Serapis at Oxyrhynchus was
       probably a forum for trading and the standard measure kept there helped to
       settle disputes.

29-30. The formula for penalty does not seem to follow the usual lines. See Berger,
        Strafklauseln.

148. APPLICATION FOR LEASE OF LAND

AM 11229   11.1 × 25.8 cm.   A. D. 172/3

This papyrus is broken in the middle and some lines may be lost though not many. For similar leases cf. Economic Survey of Roman Egypt, 74 ff. This application was apparently part of a periodic re-leasing of public land and was combined in a roll with similar applications, since traces of the ends of lines of the preceding lease are pre-served on the left. Unfortunately the terms of the new lease are lost and it cannot be determined whether the applicant bid less or more than the preceding tenant. At the end of his term of five years the applicant protects himself by the clause specifying that he cannot be held against his will on the same terms after this lease has expired. Such clauses indicate that compulsion had already been enforced and the validity of the clause was probably weakened in any period of stress or when the state had a dearth of applicants for leases of public land.

Since the rental is paid in money, the summer crops are presumably some form of garden produce.

Παρ' Ἀμμων[ίου Ἀ]πολλωνίου
τοῦ Μέλλων[ος] ἀπὸ Νικίου

βούλομαι μισθώσασθαι ἐπὶ χρόνον ἔτη πέντε ἀπὸ τοῦ ἐνεστῶτος
5 ιβ (ἔτους) εἰς θερινὰ γένη ἃς προεῖχεν
ἐν μισθώσει Βῆς Νεκθερῶτος
ἀπὸ Νήσου Μεσοποταμίας περὶ
Σένιν (ἀρούρας) β΄ καὶ π[ε]ρὶ Ψινγενι.ιβθιν
(ἄρουρα) α΄, γίν(ονται) (ἄρουραι) γ΄ ἢ ὅσαι ἐὰν ὦσι οὔ-
10 σαι ἐν κοίτῃ α΄ φόρου ἀποτάκτου
τῶν μὲν περὶ Σένιν (ἀρουρῶν) β΄ ὡς τῆς
(ἀρούρας) ἀντὶ τῶν προτελου(μένων) (δραχμῶν) ις΄
.... ξ .. β .... π[ε]ρὶ Ψινγεν ..
ιβθιν ....
15 ....
[τ]ελέσαι πλει ......
[τοῦ προκειμέ]νου φόρου, ἐὰν δὲ
αἴτιόν τι συμβῇ ‘ἢ ἀβροχήσῃ ἐγ (μέρους)’ παραδεχθῆ-
ναί μοι ὡς ἐπὶ τῶν ὁμοίων καὶ
20 μετὰ τὸν χρόνον ἄκων οὐ κατα-
σχεθήσομαι τῇ αὐτῇ μισθώσει.
(ἔτους) ιβ΄ Αὐτοκράτορος Καίσαρος Μάρκου
Αὐρηλίου Ἀντωνίνου Σεβαστοῦ Ἀρμενιακοῦ
Μηδικοῦ Παρθικοῦ Μεγίστου Θώθ κβ.
25 Ἀμμώνιος Ἀπολλωνίου ἐπιδέδωκα
ὡς πρόκ(ειται)

(2nd Hand)

καὶ ἔγραφε Δῖος δημόσιος γραφ(εύς)

(3rd Hand)

Πέτων Φέστου
Λυ(κό)πολ(ις) ιβ (ἔτους) προθειν[

"From Ammonius son of Apollonius son of Mellon residing at Nikion I wish to
lease for five years from the current 12th year for summer crops the leasehold formerly
held by Bes son of Nektheros residing at Nesus Mesopotamia consisting of 2 ar. near
Senis and 1 ar. at Psingenibthis, a total of 3 ar. or however many they may be in
sector *alpha* at a fixed rental for the 2 ar. near Senis of x dr. instead of the 16 dr.
previously paid, and likewise for the other ar. at similar terms .... nor shall I be

compelled to pay more than the aforesaid rental. If anything happens or the land is unwatered in part there shall be a rebate to me on the same terms, and after the lease expires I shall not be held against my will to the same lease. The 12th year of the emperor Caesar Marcus Aurelius Antoninus Augustus Armeniacus Medicus Parthicus Maximus. Thoth 22. I, Ammonius son of Apollonius, gave in this application as above. Written by Dius public scribe. (Countersigned) by Peton son of Festus. Lycopolis. The 12th year."

149. SALE OF LAND

A. D. 176-180

This document is in the private possession of Mr. John H. Scheide. The papyrus was folded and broken along the line of the fold on the left. About nine letters are missing at the beginning of each line, but in most cases the proper restoration can be made from the regular formulae used in documents of sale. The exact year cannot be determined since the restoration in line 13 depends on whether ἔτους was written out in full or was represented by the conventional sign of abbreviation. In any case it falls in the period of joint rule of Aurelius and Commodus.

Outright sale of land is less common than cession of property. The price of 200 dr. for 5 arouras either may indicate land of poor quality or it may be a conventional sum required for legal transfer. In 171, 11 ar. were transferred for a sum somewhat over 3,000 dr. in the Hermopolite nome (P. Ryl. 164) and somewhat earlier 4 ar. were ceded for about 800 dr. (BGU. 233, Heraclea). For prices of land in general see Economic Survey of Roman Egypt, 150 ff.

[Παρα . . . .]ς Δείου Πασίωνος ἀγορανομήσαντος τῆς Ἀρ-
σινοείτων

[πόλεως . . . . .]ι τῶι καὶ Δείω καὶ Φιλοξένω τῶ καὶ Διονυσίω
Διοσκόρου

[τοῦ καὶ . . . . .]ανου Πασίωνος ἀνχιερατεύσαντος ἀμφοτέροις

[τῆς αὐτ(ῆς) πόλ(εως) ὁμο] λογῶ κατὰ τόδε τὸ χειρόγραφον
πεπρακέναι ὑμεῖν τὰς

5 [ὑπαρχούσας] μοι περὶ κώμην Βακχιάδ[α ἐν τ]ῶ τόπω Πουατβ
λεγομένω

[ἐν μιᾶ σφ]ραγεῖδι ἀρούρας πέντε ἢ ὅσαι [ἐὰν] ὦσι τειμῆς τῆς
συμπεφω

[νημένη]ς ἀργυρίου δραχμῶν διακ[ο]σίων / ⌡ σ′ ὧν γείτονες
[καθὼς ἐκ συ]μφώνου ὑπηγορεύσαμεν ἐκ τετραγώνου σπειρο-
[μέν]ας
[καὶ αὐτόθι] ἀπεσχηκέναι ἐκ πλήρους τὴν τειμὴν βεβαιώσ[ω]
10 [πάσῃ βεβαι]ώσει ἀπὸ παντὸς τοῦ ἐπελευσομένου τὸ [δ]ὲ χειρόγραφον
[ἰδιόγραφο]ν ὑμεῖν ἐξεδόμην χωρ[ὶς] ἀλίφαδος καὶ ἐπιγρα[φῆς]
[δισσὸν γρα]φὲν κύρ[ιο]ν ἔστω ὡς ἐν δημοσίῳ κατακεχωρ[ισ-
μένον]
[(ἔτους)   ] καὶ δεκάτου Αὐρηλίων Ἀντωνείν[ο]υ καὶ Κομ-
μ[όδου]
[τῶν κυρίω]ν̄ Σεβαστῶν Ἀρμενιακῶν Μηδικῶν Πα[ρ]θικ[ῶν
Γερμανικῶν]
15 [Σαρματικῶ]ν Μεγίστων Φαῶφι ιη̄.

3. 1. ἀρχιερατεύσαντος.

"From X son of Dius, son of Pasion former agoranomus of Arsinoe to X also
known as Dius and Philoxenus also called Dionysius both sons of Dioscurus also called
...anus, son of Pasion formerly chief priest, both from the same city. I acknowledge
by this contract that I have sold to you the five arouras, or however many there may be
in one plot belonging to me at Pouatb near Bacchias at the price of 200 silver dr. as
agreed upon. The boundaries are as we have already agreed upon by square measure.
The land is under cultivation. I also acknowledge that I have received the price in full.
I shall guarantee with every guarantee your possession against every one who shall
proceed against you. This contract which I have given written in my own hand in two
copies without erasure or addition shall be valid as if recorded in public registry.
Dated in the joint rule of Antoninus and Commodus. Phaophi 18."

1-3. The names of the agoranomus and chief priest are unknown. Pasion is recorded
as chief priest in BGU 576 (II/III cent.) and Ammonius son of Claudianus
was priest before 209 (P. Hamb. 15, 16). Possibly the name Claudianus should
be restored in l. 3. Philoxenus was strategus of the Themistes-Polemon divi-
sions ca. 194-6 (BGU. 199). For these names, see Paulus, *Prosopographie der
Beamten des Arsinoites Nomos.*

5. Pouatb is otherwise unknown.

150. ABSTRACTS OF CONTRACTS

GD 7934   13 × 13 cm.   2nd century

Three fragments belong to a roll containing abstracts of contracts
recorded in a *grapheion* (cf. P. O. 1648; BGU. 1258; P. Ross. Georg.
18; Boak, Teb. Papyri, 121-128). Of these the larger contains three

columns. The first column is fairly complete, except for the beginning. It contains a settlement of ownership of catoecic land but whether by sale or by inheritance is not altogether clear. The second column is quite fragmentary and may contain a lease of land. Only the ends of a few lines are preserved from the third column, and they seem to refer to a lease of land near Berenice.

Col. 1.

]νδρειου[
κ]αὶ Μεμι[ου
]ὼς ἀπὸ[
]ωρθωτι . . . . . . (ἔτων) μς[
5 γρά]φειν καὶ . . .αφρος
]ει πέση ἐξ λ[
]τοὺς ταυτη[
π..μπ. . . . . .δου κλήρου κατοι[κικοῦ
ἀρούρας ὀκτὼ δί[μοιρον ὄγ]δοον ἐν δυσὶ σφραγ[ίσι καὶ
10 γῆς ἀμπελίτιδος [ἀρουρῶν] δύο ἀπὸ ἀρουρῶν τεσ[σάρων
τετάρτου κοι[νῶν καὶ ἀ]διαιρέτων καὶ περὶ Φ[ιλαδελ-
φείαν τρίτον μέ[ρος κοι]νὸν καὶ ἀδιαίρετον πατρι[κοῦ
ἐλαιονοπαραδείσου [ἀρουρῶ]ν τριῶν καὶ γῆς ἀμπε[λί-
τιδος ἀρο[υ]ρῶν δύο ἡμίσους τετάρτου καὶ ἄλλων [ἀρου-
15 ρῶν ἔξ λαβοῦσα παρ' αὐτοῦ ἀπαν... καὶ ἀργυρίου
δραχμὰς ὀκτακοσίας δεκαδύο [ἐκ] δὲ τῶν προκει[μέ]νων
ὑπαρχόντων ἀπεγραψάμην διὰ μὲν τῶν πρ [. . . . .
ἀνὰ τὰ προθ( )′ περὶ Ἡφαιστιάδα τ[ῆς] ἀμπ[έ]λου (ἀρούρας)
β ἀπὸ (ἀρουρῶν) δ καὶ κλή[ρου]
κατοικικοῦ (ἀρούρας) η β̄η̄ ἐν δυσὶ σφρα(γίσι) κατ' ἄγνοιαν δια-
[γεγραμ-]
20 μένας ων περὶ Φιλαδελφείαν καὶ μόνην ἡ προθετ ....
τρίτον ἀπ' ὅλω(ν) πατρικῶν κλήρου κατοικικοῦ ἀρουρῶν
τριῶν ἡμίσους αἳ διὰ τῆς μισθώσεως δηλωθ(εῖσαι) . . . .
καὶ γῆς ἀμπ[ελ]ίτιδος ἄρουραι β Γ δ καὶ ἀ[μπέλου . . . .
καὶ ὑποδοχῆς (ἄρουραι) δ δ̄ η̄ ῑς λο ξ̄ο διὰ δευτέρου
25 ἐπιδίδωμι τόδε τὸ ὑπόμνημα . . . .
. . . . . . .ἀμφ]οτέρων ἐπερρωτηθέντων ὡμολογήσαντο

Col. 2.

] καὶ Πτολεμαίῳ Πετεβ[

] Λογγινίας Νιγερεα Ν[

τ]ου αὐτὴ καταγινομένη(?) [

]λιου καὶ Σεράνου ....ἐγραφ.....[

5   ]ν βιβλιοφύλακος δὲ ἀγοραστικοῦ παρὰ[

[κλ]ήρου κατοικικοῦ ἀρούρας [εἴ]κοσι δ[ί]μοιρον

καὶ γῆς ἀμπελίτιδος ἀρούρας δύ[ο ἥ]μισου ἀπὸ τ[εσσαρῶν

κοινῶν]

καὶ ἀδιαιρέτων περὶ κώμην Ἡφαιστιάδα .....

..οντο... Μάρκῳ Πετρωνίῳ ου..........

10   το]ῦ Μάρκου Πετρωνίου ..δ .....

ὀφείλων ... ἐκ τούτου ...

ματι σὴν μίσθωσιν ἀργυρίου δραχμὰς ...

.. πρὸς τὸν διὰ τῆς μισθώσεως ἐὰν ...

151. LEASE OF SLAVES

AM 11246   14.5 × 15 cm.   341 or later

Interesting legal points are raised by this document. The lease is unique in that the rental of the slaves is paid in wheat and not in money. The slaves are called ἀθάνατοι (l. 7) and this is explained later on (ll. 13-15) by the statement that if the slaves die during the term of the lease the loss is made good by the lessee. Finally the *partus* of the slaves became the property of the lessee rather than of the lessor to whom they would naturally belong by Roman law. In Republican times the ownership was disputed. Thus Cicero (de finibus, I. 4. 12) says: An partus ancillae sitne in fructu habendus disseretur inter principes civitatis, P. Scaevolam, M'. que Manilium, ab iisque M. Brutus dissentiet. In the Empire, however, the matter was beyond dispute and Gaius (Dig. 22. 1. 28) is quoted as saying: Partus vero ancillae in fructu non est itaque ad dominum proprietatis pertinet. Neither the usufructuary nor the bonae fidei possessor had ownership of the offspring, and it is certain that the lessee could have no legal claim unless special provision was made for it (Buckland, Roman Law of Slavery, 21 ff.).

The purpose of the lessee can only be surmised. He may have been engaged in breeding slaves for commercial purposes, or he may be the keeper of a brothel. The rental seems rather low, but this may be due to famine conditions, to the risks which fell on the lessee, or to other causes. For leases and sales of slaves in Egypt, see Economic Survey of Roman Egypt, 277 ff.

Αὐρήλιοι Πετιρε[ι]ῳ καὶ Λυκαρ[ιωνι]
Λυκαριωνος ἀπ[ὸ] β(ενε)φ(ικιαρίων) δι Ἀπ[ο]λλιν[αρίου]
προνοητοῦ παρὰ Αὐρηλίο[υ]
Διοσκόρου ἀπὸ κώμης Ἰβίωνο(ς)
5 βούλομαι μισθώσασθαι παρ' ὑμῶν ἐκ
τῶν ὑπαρχόντων ὑμῖν [τ]ὰς δύο
ἀθανάτου[ς] μία μὲν τελείαν φυρὰν
ὀνόματι Εἰσά[ρ]ιον ἡ δὲ ἑτέρα δ[.]. ις λευ-
κὴ ὀνόματι Τεσευρις ἐπὶ χρόνο[ν] ἐνιαυ-
10 τὸν ἕνα ἀπὸ τοῦ ὄντος μην[ὸ]ς Ἀθὺρ ιε/
ἰνδικτίονος φόρου κατ' ἔτος ἔκαστον
πυροῦ ἀρτάβα[ς] ἑξ (ἀρτάβας) ς' τὸν δὲ φόρον [ἀ]ποδώσω
κατ' ἔτος ἔκα[σ]τον ἐπὰν δὲ ὃ μὴ γίνη-
το θάνατος ἐκβῇ ὄντος πρὸς ἐμὲ
15 τὸν μισθούμενον τῆς δὲ τούτων
γονῆς οὔσης πρὸς τὸν α[ὐ]τὸν μισ
θούμενον [κ]αὶ τῆς τούτων θρ[έ]ψ[εως]
καὶ πάση[ς ἐ]πιμελείας καὶ μετὰ τὸν
[χρόνον · — — — — —

1. 1. Αὐρηλίοις
7. 1. τελεία πυρρά
13. 1. γίνοιτο, or γένοιτο: cf. Mayser I. 81

"To the Aurelii Petirius and Lycarion sons of Lycarion former beneficiarii through their agent Apollinarius from Aurelius Dioscurus resident in the village of Ibion. I wish to lease from you two slaves belonging to you, one full-grown, blonde named Isarion, the other .... white, named Teseuris on terms of replacement in case of loss for one year from the current month Hathyr in the 15th indiction at a yearly rental of six artabas of wheat and I shall pay the rental yearly. If death occurs, which I pray may not happen, the loss falls upon me the lessee. The offspring of these slaves also belongs to the lessee and their care and entire maintenance falls upon him. After the lease expires I shall return the slaves in good condition etc."

7. ἀθανάτους. This term is sometimes used in connection with flocks, and in the case of a lease implies that the lessee will return the flock without impairment in size.

8. The descriptive epithet is difficult to restore. Probably not more than two letters are missing, and though δμωίς seems the obvious restoration, it does not suit the traces of ink still visible, and this term is not likely in commercial transactions.

C. ACCOUNTS AND MISCELLANEOUS DOCUMENTS

152. Accounts

AM 8915 *verso*   31 × 23 cm.   A. D. 55-60

The *recto* contains an account of taxes (P. Princeton 53). The writing on the left half of Col. I has been erased by exposure to sand blasts. The scribe wrote an illegible cursive and many of the entries are difficult to decipher. The record of the second year contains expenditures for wages and other expenses while the first three entries in Col. II record expenses for the month of Mesore. The accounts of the third year deal only with expenditures for the purchase of wool, hay, and seed. The last three lines contain accounts of the seventh year. Since these accounts were recorded by the same hand and apparently at the same time, they possibly represent notes jotted down on this piece of scrap paper in preparing a report of the estate for a five-year period. See Economic Survey of Roman Egypt, 174 ff. for farm accounts in Roman times.

Col. 1

δαπάν]ης ὑπὲρ Μαλίου μεγάλου `κ´
                    ]καὶ μητρὸς   τοῦ β (ἔτους)
[Νέρωνος τοῦ] κυρίου
                    ]υριωι εἰς κοπήν
5   ]τας   ʃ μη
                    ]αγγινο(ν)
                    ] …οας ἡμισείας   ʃ θ
[Πνεφερῶ]τει ποιμένι μισθοῦ
[μηνῶν] δ   ʃ ξδ

10   ]καὶ ἐργάτου   α   ʃ γ

    ]στικου   ʃ γ

    ]'Ἀρταβίας {ʃ λη (ἔτους)} β (ἔτους)   ʃ λϛ ʃ

    ]αντιου .... τῆς αὐτῆ(ς) μητρὸ(ς) δ....   ʃ ι

    Π]νεφέρωτο(ς) καὶ Καλίο(υ) αὐτῶ(ν)   ʃ ε

15   ]καὶ ὑπὲρ ὑφαντίου   ʃ ε

Col. 2

Μεσορηι Πονώρει Ἐππίο(υ) Πᾶβις   ʃ σμη

  ... λωρη( )   ʃ ρμ

κατὰ ...ετας ὑπὲρ δαπάνης   ʃ πε ʃ

(ἔτους) γ Νέρωνος τοῦ κυρίου

5 ἀνήλωσις

Νεμείωνει Τιτάνου ʿωʹ τιμῆ(ς) τιμῆ(ς) πόκωω(ν)(sic)   ʃ ξ

τειμῆ(ς) πόκος (sic) παρὰ Θέωνο(ς) υἱ⟨ο⟩ῦ   ʃ ε

    παρὰ Φιλήμονος   δ   ʃ ιϛ

    σπόρω(ν) γ (ἔτους)

10 τειμῆς χόρτου χλωροῦ διὰ Ἀπολλῶτος

Σκρίπου   {ἀργ(υρίου) ʃ τδ}   ʃ σ[

    τειμῆς χλωρῶν καὶ σπόρο(υ)   ʃ [ ]

    τειμῆς σπερμάτων ϛπερματο...... {τ..}

ἐὰν θελ.( )

15   ζ (ἔτους)   ζ (ἔτους)

Θύωνει Ταβουρίωι τειμῆς χόρτου ἰς κοπ(ὴν)[ ]

Πνεφερῶτι ποιμένει μηνὸς. [ ]

Col. 1. 1. Above the final letter of μεγάλου is superscribed a letter resembling *kappa* possibly κ(τήματος). Cf. II. 6 where *omega* is superscribed over the patronymic.

    12. The reading Ἀρταβίας seems certain and the entry in the following line indicates that the name of the mother should be read here. The tax *artabeia* was never paid in money (Wallace, Taxation in Roman Egypt, *s. v.*).

Col. 2. 1. Πᾶβις, a proper name in this position seems unlikely. Possibly πόκοις should be read.

    2. This entry is preceded by a long slanting stroke usually used to indicate a total. The reading is plain enough and I have indicated the letters as they appear, but the meaning is unintelligible.

    6-8. The purchase of wool seems to indicate some commercial weaving on the estate. Cf. I. 15 where payment is made for a weaving establishment.

    15. A marginal entry apparently by the same scribe who made the record.

153. ORDER FOR WINE

AM 11226   6.5 × 13.5 cm.   2nd or 3rd century

ἀνυξάτωσαν τὸ σκρή-
νιον καὶ δότωσάν
σοι τὸ παρακλεί-
διον τοῦ πυλῶνος
5 κ᾽ ἔσται ἔν τῶ πυλῶ-
νι οἴνου (τετρά)χ(οα) ιθ (δί)χ(οα) η
ἐν τῶ πρώτω ἀγωγίω
ἠνέχθη σοι (τετρά)χ(οα) σπη
χ(αίρειν)

l. 1. ἀνοιξάτωσαν

" Have them open the bureau and give you the key of the gate house. There will be 19 jars holding 4 choes and 8 holding 2 choes. In the first cargo 288 4-choes jars were brought to you. Farewell."

154. CONTRACT

GD 7617   10.5 × 7 cm.   A. D. 545

Acknowledgment of receipt of a gold solidus as advance payment of a contract made by the dung-carrier Christodorus with Prasutis. Either the post-consular date or the year of the indiction is wrong. The former belongs to the year 545 and the document is dated September 7 when the ninth indiction had just begun. Where there is a conflict between the two systems of dating, the indiction is usually wrong.

τοῖς τὸ δ μετὰ τὴν ὑπατίαν Φλαουίου
Βασιλίου τοῦ λαμπρ(οτάτου) Θὼθ ι ἰνδ(ικτίονος)
Αὐρήλιος Χριστόδωρος ὀνθομεταφόρ(ος)
υἱὸς Φὶβ μητρὸς Ἡραΐδος ἀπὸ τῆς
5 Ὀξυρυγχιτῶν Αὐρηλίω Πρασῦτι κριβανεῖ υἱῶ
Βίκτορος ἀπὸ τῆς αὐτῆς πόλεως
χαίρειν. ὁμολογῶ ἐσχηκέ[ναι] παρ[ά] σου ἐντεῦθεν
ἤδη λόγω προτελείας τοῦ ἐμοῦ μισθοῦ

χρυσοῦ νομισμάτιον ἕν, ἐφ᾽ ὧτ᾽ ἐμὲ
10 ἐμβῆναι εἰς τὸ σὸν ὀνάριον πρὸς

. . . .

Verso

συνάλλαγμα   τ[   ]

5. κριβανεῖ = κλιβανεῖ

155. ACCOUNTS

AM 11224 B   3 × 6 cm.   2nd or 3rd century

A useful survey of the drug trade in ancient times may be found in Schmidt, Drogen und Drogenhandel im Altertum.

Recto		
παιδικ(ά)		
χαλκ(οῦ) κεκαυμ(ένου)	∫ δ	
καδμίας	∫ ση	
ὀπίου	∫ κϛ	
5 ζμυρναίας	∫ β	
ἐρίκας Καρί(ας)	∫ β	
ἀκακίας	∫ σ	
κομμ( )	∫ σ	
ὕδωρ ✳		
10 πίπερ γλυθὺ τὸ		
πάχος		

Verso		
στατίω(ν) πρὸς Φλα( )		
πέπερ μου	∫ β	
λιθάργ(ου)	∫ β	
ζμυρναίας	∫ δ	
5 πιάρματος	∫ β	
κόμματος	∫ ι	
οἴνου ✳ το κομ( )		
καὶ ἐπιβάλοντα		

R. 1. παιδικά. The meaning of this in connection with the purchase of drugs listed below is uncertain. The corresponding entry on the *Verso* seems to imply a location.

2. χαλκοῦ κεκ. See Galen XII. 242 for uses.

6. ἐρίκας Καρί[ας]. Apparently new in ancient trade in drugs.

8. κομμ( ). Probably the same as in *V*. l. 6, and evidently not the same as κόμμι or the gum derived from the acacia tree (Theophrastus, H. Plant. 9. 1. 3).

9. The sign following ὕδωρ is that often used for the Roman denarius. A similar sign is found in *V*. l. 7 following οἴνου.

10. γλυθύ. Probably γλυκύ, but the following phrase does not help to elucidate its meaning. Interchange of θ and κ is not elsewhere attested.

V. 5. πιάρματος. πῖαρ is apparently indeclinable in Classic Greek.

6. κόμματος. See *R*. l. 8.

156. Money-order

GD 7736 A   12.0 × 6.0 cm.   Dec. 3, A. D. 302

π(αρὰ) Ψεναμούνιος Ἀτίωνι ἀρτοκόπ(ῳ) χαίρειν
Δὸς Ἀπολλωνίῳ ἀφ' ὧν ἔχεις ὑπὲρ τιμῆς σίτου
ἀργυρίου δραχμὰς χιλείας ἑκατόν
                              (γίνονται) Ἀρ
5 (ἔτους) ιη/ καὶ ιζ/ καὶ ι/ Χοίακ ζ' ἔρρωσο.

" Psenamounis greets Atio, the baker. Pay Apollonius from the funds in your possession 1,100 dr. in silver for grain. Date.

1. ἀρτοκόπ(ῳ). This is probably to be restored in P. Lond. 604 A, 57 and P. Lond. 604 B, 116.

5. Read ιϠ/. The 18th year of Diocletian ended Nov. 16, 302, or about two weeks before this order was issued.

157. List of Names

GD 7929 B + 7935 C   9 × 14 cm.   4th century

Lines 1-3 are on 7935 C, and 4-8 on 7929 B. The two pieces undoubtedly belong together, for the hand and the texture of the papyrus are identical in both. There may have been a gap between them, or they may have fitted closely together; but the break does not fit, so they could not have been in actual contact. The form Παταησίου of the genitive in line 5 is new.

εἰσὶν τὰ ὀνόματα
Ἀφύγχις Χωοῦτος
Παπτῆβε Πετίριος

Νεῖ[λος . . .].λυτος
5 Ἀπφοῦς Παταησίου
Ἀμόϊς Παύλου
Παμουν Νικίου
Ἀπίων Θέωνος

158. LIST OF FARMS

GD 7926 A   8.6 × 14.8 cm.   6th century

This list resembles P. Iand 51; but, since it is called a λόγος, numbers probably followed the names.

$$- - - \text{traces} - - -$$

λόγ(ος) ἐπὶ τῆς β ἰνδ(ικτίονος)
   οὕτως
χωρίου προαστίου
5 Σκέλους
Τρίγου
Νοτινοῦ
Καλουρίας
μηχ(άν)η[ς] Φαησερῶ
10 Ἀδαίου
Νεπ( )
Κοτυλεείου
Ταρουσέβτ'
Νήσου Λευκαδίου
15 Ἀντιπέλης

5. P. Oxy. 998; P. Iand. 21; BGU. 693 (cf. 960); P. Kl. Form. 1107; SPP. X. 73, 80, 87, 124, 149, 239, 282, 285.

6. P. Iand. 51; cf. Τριγήου, P. Oxy. 1911, which, however, cannot be read here.

7. P. Oxy. 1911.

8. SB. 1989e; cf. SPP. X. 198.

9. Not otherwise attested; possibly read Φανσερῶ.

10. P. Oxy. 136, 139, 685, 747, 1285; cf. P. Oxy. 989.

11. Not otherwise known. Possibly read Νεοῦ, but not Νεο(φ)ύ(του), SB. 1973. 20.

12. P. Oxy. 1911; cf. SB. 1973. 16.

13. P. Oxy. 998, 1911.

14. P. Oxy. 134, 1637, 1659; P. Princ. 88.

15. Ἀντι(πέρας) Πέλης might be read (P. Oxy. 1637, 1659), but there is nothing to indicate that this is an abbreviation.

D. MAGIC PAPYRUS

159. FEVER AMULET

AM 11230   14 × 6 cm.   3rd or 4th century

This charm is written on very cheap paper by an unlettered hand. The papyrus is a palimpsest and had evidently been folded into small compass presumably to be placed in a small cylinder and worn on the body of the patient (cf. Wilcken, Archiv I, 420 ff.). The pattern exhibited in this charm is known as βοτρυοειδῶς. The two other common patterns, formed by dropping a letter in successive lines from either right or left ends and giving the effect of a right triangle, are known as πτερυγοειδῶς. Magical papyri are collected by Preisendanz, Papyri Graecae Magicae, Die Griechischen Zauberpapyri.

The superstitious use of amulets and charms, so prevalent in the ancient world (Pliny, N. H. XXVIII. 3 discusses whether verba et incantamenta carminum possess any efficacy, cf. Lucian, Philopseudes, 78), was no doubt, to judge from repeated remonstrance against them, also prevalent in the early Church (Eusebius, Demonstratio evangelica. III, 6 in Migne, Pat. Gr., XXII, 226; Augustine, De doctrina Christiana, II, xxix, 45 in Migne, Pat. Lat. XXXIV, 56 f.). The Synod of Laodicea (A. D. 342-381, Hefele, History of the Councils, II, 298) issued a separate canon proscribing the manufacture and use of amulets: ". . . and those who wear such (φυλακτήρια) we command to be cast out of the Church" (Nicene and Post-Nicene Fathers, second series, XIV, p. 151). In later ages Christians wore arculae, containing bits of the remains of saints suspended around the neck (Vita Gregorii Magni, IV, 80. See Ducange, Glossarium, s. vv. encolpium, phylacterium).

ζαγουρ[η]παγουρη

αγουρηπαγουρ

γουρηπαγου

ουρηπαγο

5   υρηπαγ

ρηπα

ηπ

▣

κύριοι ἄγγελοι

10 καὶ ἀγαθὴ παύ-
σαται [. .]διαν ὃν
ἔτεκεν [Σ]οφία
ἀπὸ τ[οῦ] ἀνέ-
χοντος αὐτὸν
15 πυρετοῦ ἐν τῇ
σήμερον ἡμέρα
ἐν τῇ ἄρτι ὥρα
[ἤδη ἤ]δη τα-
[χὺ τα]χύ.

10. ἀγαθὴ l. ἀγαθοί; παύσαται l. παύσατε

"Good angels who rule over us allay the fever of ..dias, whom Sophia bore, this very day this very hour and this very moment at once at once.

1. ζαγουρη. Cf. P. Lond. 47, 480; Wessely, Ephesia Grammata, nos. 36, 206 f., 209, 335; PGM. XXXVI, 10, 64, 309, 350. παγουρη is less common, cf. P. Lond. 121, ll. 597, 606; PGM. XXXVI, 309 (Eitrem in P. Oslo 1 read πατουρη), 350. Concerning the triangular form see also Kropatschek, de amuletorum apud antiquos usu, p. 29. Iamblichus answers Porphyry's question in the latter's epistle to the Egyptian Anebo as to why charms and incantations are couched in barbaric and outlandish words, by replying that they lose their potency (δύναμις) if translated (De mysteriis, vii, 5).

8. Apparently designed as a ligature of the two letters in the preceding line.

9. The identity of the angels invoked may with some degree of probability be inferred from similar charms and from apocryphal and pseudepigraphical literature where such names are found as Arlaph, Azael, Arakiel, Gabriel, Michael, Phanual, Raphiel, Raguel, Ramiel, Samiel, Sariel, Uriel, etc. (Schlumberger, REG. V (1892) 76 ff.; Dorigny, ibid. IV (1891), 288; Sibylline Oracles, II, 214 (Rzach); Enoch, chaps. xx, xl; Apocalypse of Baruch (Syriac) lv, 3; Apocalypse of Moses 2; IV Ezra, iv, 36 (cf. Charles, The Apocrypha and Pseudepigrapha, II, 567). κύριοι is usually used to address the deity invoked by the suppliant (Wünsch, Arch. f. Rel. XII (1909), 38. Dietrich equates ἄγγελοι with δαίμονες (Nekyia, 2nd ed.), 60 f.

11. The name, apparently masculine, cannot be determined. There is space in the lacuna for one broad or two narrow letters. Only the tops of the next two letters are visible and they may be read as δρ, αρ, or λι.

12. In the magical papyri maternal rather than paternal relationships predominate, e.g. PMG. XLIII, 5b, P. O. 1275. The only clear case of a patronymic is in a curse tablet from Cumae (Audollent, Defixionum—Tabellae, 198), but cf. Winter, Michigan Papyri, III, 155.

18. This reiteration expresses the urgency of the suppliant in demanding help (cf. Wessely, op. cit. 176; PGM. XVIIIb, XXXVI, 11, 84, 113 f., 132, 319 f., 360, XXXIX, l. 21). Wilcken (Archiv, I, 426) remarks that ταχὺ ταχύ was a popular formula in Greek amulets and was taken over not only into similar Coptic texts but also into Latin, adducing tacs tacs in CIA, Appendix "Defixionum Tabellae Atticae, p. xxviii, which Wünsch conjectures to be ταχέως ταχέως. So Paul, ad Gal. 1, 8, repeats the imprecation ἀνάθεμα ἔστω.

E. PRIVATE CORRESPONDENCE

160. LETTER

GD 7680   12 × 10.5 cm.   Last 1st century B. C.

For the form of salutation, cf. Exler, A Study in Greek Episto-
lography, 105 ff.

Παρὰ Σ[. . . .] ᾿Αγχασίωι καὶ Θαμίνει χαίρειν
καὶ ἐρρ[ῶσ]θαι. ἔρρωμαι δὲ καὶ αὐτός. γεγράφαμεν
Πνεφ[ε]ρῶτι ὅπως δὴ αἰτῆι συγγραφήν.
καλῶς [οὖ]ν ποιήσεις κομίσα⟨ς⟩ καὶ ἔχε μέχρι
5 τοῦ ἐ[μὲ π]αραγενέσθαι.

Verso

γυναῖκα Κολάνου   ᾿Αγχασίωι

"From *x* to Anchasius and Thamines greeting and good health. I also am well.
I have written to Pnepheros to demand a contract. You will do well to get it and
keep it safe until I come."

161. LETTER

AM 11232   9 × 23 cm.   A. D. 33

Chaeremon is evidently the owner of considerable property and his
order to send guards to two different places about the middle of
November implies that these lots were planted in vineyards.

Χ[αιρήμω]ν Δίωι χαίρε(ιν)
καὶ ὑγ[ιαί]νειν. οὐδέν
μοι ἔγραψας περὶ ὧν
σοι ἔγ[ρα]ψα. τὸ λοιπὸν
5 οὖν [πέμψ]ον φύλακα
εἰ ἔχ[εις ..] τον εἰς τὸ
νεόφυτον πατρικὸν
καὶ εἰ ἔχεις καὶ εἰς τὸν
᾿Αρεί[ο]ν. [πέμ]ψον

10 καὶ μὴ ἐκεῖ ἀποτά-
ξης ἕως σοι γράψωι
τὰ δ' ἄλλ' εὖ γ(ίνεται). ἔρρωσ(ο)
(ἔτους) ιθ' Τιβερίου Καίσαρος
μηνὸ[ς Νέου Σεβαστο]ῦ κ̄ᾱ.

15 Αρ.....................
μυσθο[ῦ .... τ]ὸν ἴδι[ον]

Verso

Ἀπόδος   Δίωι

" Chaeremon sends greetings and wishes for good health to Dius. You have never answered my letter. Well then send a trustworthy(?) guard to the new orchard on your father's property and if you have another send him also to the place of Areius. Send them and keep them there until I write. Everything else is going well. Farewell. The 19th year of Tiberius Caesar, the 21st of New August."

6. Not much more than two or possibly three letters are to be restored in the lacuna preceding τον. Possibly [πισ]τόν.

9. An Ἀρείου ἐποίκιον is known but the masculine article at the end of line 8 implies that some such word as τόπος is to be understood. I have restored πέμψον at the end of line 9 with some hesitation. The letters on the papyrus seem to be ψοσι but for this no satisfactory restoration seems possible.

15-16. Chaeremon apparently added a postscript but the writing has been almost completely erased, and the papyrus has been torn at the end of line 16.

162. LETTER

GD 7535 *verso*   11.8 × 16 cm.   A. D. 89/90

......αυ ...ην........υο
[τ]ῆς πεντεκαιδεκάτης α...α...
[κα]ὶ ἐπεὶ βουλῇ εἶμι εἰς Ἀλεξ-
[άν]δρειαν. πλεῦσαι μετέωρόν μου
5 [λιπώ]ν· μὴ οὖν ἄλλως ποιήσης.
[γρά]φε ἐπεὶ ἕως τῆς εἰκάδος
[...]κ .. γείνομαι ἐὰν δὲ μὴι
[θέλω]σί μὲ ταῦτα ποιεῖν γράψον
[μοι] αὔριον εἴνα ὠδῖνα μὴ ποιήση.
10 ἐὰν δέ μοι μ[εῖ]ζον θελήσης

παρασχεῖν ὅλας τρεῖς μοι ποιήσεις
ἔση μοι οὖν μεγάλην μοι χάριτα
παρεσχημένος τοῦτο ποιήσας
ἐρρῶσθαι [εὔχο]μαι.
15 (ἔτους) θ Δομιτιανοῦ τοῦ κυρίου μηνὸς Γερμανικοῦ ια

"(I arrived?) on the fifteenth, ... and since you wish I will go to Alexandria. Do you set sail yourself leaving my business unfinished(?) Do not fail. Write me since I am at ...... until the 20th. If they do not want me to do these things write me tomorrow lest he cause me anguish. If you are willing to do more for me, you will make me three whole ones. In doing this you will do me a great favor. Farewell. The 9th year of Domitian, our lord. Germanicus 11th."

4. πλεῦσαι. The middle imperative is unusual, but some command is necessary. μετέωρον. Cf. P. O. 238 for a discussion of the meaning of this word. Apparently used here as a noun with the personal pronoun depending on it. It may be noted that this writer uses the personal pronoun somewhat excessively.

163. Letter

GD 7529   13 × 8 cm.   2nd century

This letter had been folded across lines 4 and 8 with the result that the fibre has been broken and the letters are now much blurred. Horion was apparently the stable manager of a camel-transport system. The address on the *verso* might imply that Gaius was the owner but his demand for the value of a lost article seems to place him as a shipper, possibly a veteran soldier engaged in business.

Γαῖος Ὠρίωνι τῷ φιλτάτῳ χαίρειν.
καὶ ἄλλοτέ σοι ἔγραψα διὰ τοῦ καμηλείτου σου
ὅτι οὐδείς μοι δέδωκε τοῦ χόος τῆς κεδρίας
διὸ ἐὰν μὲν ἐπανακλίνῃς, εὖ καὶ καλῶς·
5 εἰ δὲ μὴ ἐντελήσῃ τῷ καμηλείτῃ σου ὅπως
δοῖ μοι ἢ τὴν τιμὴν ἢ σιτάρια αὐτῶν
ἀλλὰ μὴ ἀμελήσῃς καὶ γράψις ἡμῖν περὶ τῶν
Ἀμμωνίου σκέων ψιλῶν καὶ ....πνι ἔδοκε
καὶ ἡ ἐπιστολὴ τοῦ υἱοῦ αὐτοῦ.
10   ἔρρωσο
                          Φαμενὼθ κη′

Verso

Ὠ[ρί]ωνι καμηλείτ[η]   εἰς τὸν καμηλ(είτην) αὐτοῦ
ἀπὸ Γαΐου

" Gaius greets his dearest Horion. I have already written you by the hand of your camel-driver that no one has delivered the pint of cedar oil. Wherefore if you return(?) it, well and good, but if not, you will instruct the camel-driver either to give me the value or their grain. But do not neglect it, and you will write to us about the light baggage of Ammonius and . . . ., also the letter of his son. Farewell. Phamenoth 28."

4. ἐπανακλίνης. This suits the traces of the letters, but does not give a satisfactory meaning. ἐπανακομίσης is too long and ἐπανακρίνης cannot be read, though possibly there is a metathesis of ρ for λ, cf. Mayser, Grammatik I. 188.

5. ἐντελήση. Apparently the future middle of ἐντέλλω.

6. αὐτῶν. Nothing in the letter indicates to whom this refers or why Gaius should receive their grain. Were the drivers penalized for failure to make proper delivery by forfeiture of their grain allowance? It is possible that ἢ σιτάρια should be read as ἰς σιτάρια but if so, there is no correlative for ἢ τὴν τιμήν.

8. ..πνι. Possibly τινι, but it does not seem possible to read ὧτινι.

9. ἡ ἐπιστολή. Apparently to be loosely construed with περί.

164. LETTER

AM 11226 B *verso*   6.8 × 10.5 cm.   2nd century

Χαιρήμων Σαραπάμ-
μων[ι] τῷ ἀδελφῷ χαίρειν.
καλῶς ποιήσεις κἂν νῦ[ν]
δοὺς τῷ νομοφύλακι τὴν
5 διαγραφὴν εἰδὼς τὴν ἀν-
νάνκην τοῦ μηνιαίου,
καὶ σὺν θεῷ ἐὰν δυ[ν]ώμ[ε]θα
ἐκπλέξωμεν αὐτὸ χωρὶς
μάχης, ἐρρῶσθαί σε εὔ-
10 χομαι.

5-6. 1. ἀνάγκην: dittography caused by dividing word at end of line.

8. Cf. P Ross-Georg. III. 1. 11 ; III. 3. 3, note.

" Chaeremon greets his brother Sarapammon. You will do well right now by giving the report to the nome-guard since you are aware of the necessity of the monthly statement and with God's help if we can let us confound him without a fight. Farewell."

8. Outwitting the officials seems a favorite pursuit of the Egyptian. See P. Tebt. 315.

165. Letter

AM 11234   16 × 7 cm.   2nd century

A gentle reminder to a friend of an approaching birthday.

χαίροις Ὠρίω[νι]
πέμψον
ἡμεῖν αὔ-
ριον ἥ ἐσ-
5 τιν τεσσα-
ρεσκαιδεκά-
τη ἰχθύδι-
ον δαψιλάς.
οιῖδας γὰρ
10 ὅτι κυρία
ἐστὶ ἡ γένε-
σις. ἐρρῶσ(θαι)
ιγ'

8. δαψιλάς l. δαψιλές.
9. οιῖδας l. οῖδας.

"Greetings to Horion. Send me tomorrow, the 14th, a tasty fish. For you know that it is my official birthday. Farewell. The 13th."

166. Letter

AM 11225 A   10.4 × 12.5 cm.   2nd or 3rd century

This letter is written on the *verso*. The writing on the *recto* was erased and the address written across the lines. The letter was folded before the ink was dry and the blots have increased the difficulty of deciphering a very illegible hand.

The request to guard the body is unusual. According to Diodorus (I. 92-3) a body which was pledged as security for a loan remained unburied until the debt was discharged. For this practice the papyri offer no evidence, and there is no indication of any such purpose here. Mr. Youtie suggests that the protection of the body against mutilation until proper burial was part of the primitive Egyptian cult and refers to J. G. Frazer, The Fear of the Dead in Primitive Religion.

Verso

Βησᾶς χρυσοχοῦς Εἰδῶς
πολλὰ χαίρειν. ἀσπάζομαί
σε πολλὰ μετὰ τῶν τέκνω(ν)
σου. κόμισον τὸν πατέρα
5 μου τὸν νεκρὸν καὶ ἀσφά-
λισον ἕως ἂν σὺν θεῶ
ἀναπλεύσω εἰς ἐκφορά[ν]. δώ-
σις οἰκείως. οὐ πάλιν
ἀμελὶς ὑπὲρ κτήσεως. εἰς ἄλ-
10 λην ἡμ[έρα]ν τὸ σῶμα θάψῃς.
ἐρρῶσθαί σε εὔχομαι.

Recto

Εἰδῶς ἀ(πὸ) Βησᾶς χρυ-
σοχοῦς.

"Besas the goldsmith sends many greetings to Eidos. I pay my respects to you and to your children. Fetch the body of my father and keep it safe until I sail back, God willing, to the funeral. You will make a gift in friendly fashion. You are not again neglectful of the property. On another day you will bury the body. I pray for your health."

1. Εἰδῶς is indeclinable.

9. κτήσεως. Does this refer to the possession of the body or to property in general?

This formula in the address is rare. See Ziermann, de epistularum Graecarum formulis solemnibus.

167. LETTER

AM 11238   8 × 8.5 cm.   3rd century

Αὐρήλιος Ἐριεῦς Αὐρηλίω
Τ.ρυ...νει τῶ ἀδελφῶ
χαίρειν. πρὸ μὲν πάντων
εὔχομαί σε ὑγένειν καὶ τὸ
5 προσκύνημά σου ποιῶ πρὸς
τοῖς πατρώοις θεοῖς καθὼς
ἐνέτειλάς μοι. περὶ τῆς θυγατρὸς

ἀμέριμνος γενοῦ. μὴ ἀμελή-
σης περὶ ὧν σοι ἐνετειλάμην.
10 ἐὰν μαθῆς ὅτι δυνατὸν ἀγο-
ράσαι ἄλλην μνᾶν ὡς τὰ
ἄλλα, ἀγόρασον. ὡς ἐλθ.....
θενιο................

"From Aurelius Herieus to his brother Aurelius ..... greetings. Above all I pray for your health and I offer prayers for you before our ancestral gods as you bade me. Do not worry about your daughter. Don't forget about my instructions to you. If you find you can buy another mina at the same rate as the others, buy. ...."

168. LETTER

AM 11228 B   10.5 × 5.5 cm.   3rd or 4th century

This seems to be the letter of an illiterate person. Written in uncials rather poorly formed, it may be a boy's scribbling.

Νέστωρ ἡ γυνὴ αὐτοῦ πᾶν ποίησον μὴ ἀμ[ηλήσῃς
ποίησον μὴ ἀμηλήσῃς ναῦλος ε[
Ζωείλου καὶ ἐγὼ διδῶ τὸν ναῦλον[
απα οὖν ἤτει πᾶν ποίησον αἴτησον[
5 σιν μαι.

"Nestor to his wife. Do everything. Don't neglect it....... Do everything. Don't neglect it. The fare..... of Zoilus. Let me pay the fare...... he was asking. Do everything. Ask ...."

169. LETTER

GD 7526   20 × 13.5 cm.   5th century

If the restoration proposed in l. 3 is correct, this letter seems to be written to the father of a young lady by a suitor.

τῷ δεσπότῃ μ[ου
καὶ τῷ εὐγένει χαρακτῆρει τῆς θαυ[
αὐτῇ τῇ πίρα ἐραστὴς γεγένημαι τῆς σῆς θ[υγατρὸς[
τὴν σὴν ἀρετὴν καθ' ἃ χρεωστεῖται τοῖς ε.[

5 μεμνημένος τῆς σῆς ἑτερίας ἀπαιτῶν[
  διάθεσιν ἐπειτ[

Verso

τῷ δεσπότη μου ὡς ἀλη[θῶς]

170. LETTER

GD 7688   16.5 × 12.5 cm.   6th century

To judge by the position of π(αρά) about half is lost in each line.

                                        π(αρὰ)

† ἐκέλευσεν ὁ ἐμὸς δεσπότης ὅτι πέμπω διὰ τὰ καμήλ[ια
  οὐκ ἐπέμψατε καννῦν καταξιώσατε πέμψαι δι᾽ αὐ[τῶν...
  εἰς ταύτην τὴν κώμην καὶ ἔλαβεν ἄλλα καμήλια [...
  μὴ οὖν ἀμελήσατε τὸ παραυτὰ πέμψαι δι᾽ αὐτα ἐπι...
5 ἐπὶ τοῦ παρόντος τάδε κέντρια τοῦ ὀκνολαδ..[...
  παραυτὰ καταξιώσατε πέμψαι τόδε πιτ᾽τάκιο[ν....
  καταξιώσατε πέμψαι ἵνα λάβω τὸ ὁλοκότ᾽τινο[ν
  ....τὸ πιτ᾽τάκ[ιον.........
  .... τὸ ὁλοκότ᾽τινον παραυτὰ κ.[..

Verso

  † ἀπόδος Ἱλαριτα....

DESCRIPTIONS

171. (Inv. nos. GD 7736 B; 7734 B). 1st century. Two small fragments written in large uncials may be literary fragments.

```
]οιτην φ[                    ]..ηλοτ[
]τ έσχε βα[                  ]έρριπτο[
]ρουντες[                   ]οργως π[
]οιπον οφ[                  ]ενατατο[
5  ]ς οπτον[              5  ]αγορευοντ[
]ητηι[                      ]οτάτοις ο[
]ουτω[                      ]ευον αιρε[
τ]υφλον[                    ].νοντα[
].αι κω[                    ]ῶ φίλτατε[
10 ]μεν..[             10  ]ἀνὰ τὸν π[
                            ]ἐχθρῶν αυ[
                            ]ς καὶ δοτ[
                            ]σου θεις[
```

172. (Inv. no. AM 11233. 15 × 20 cm.). Survey of land (cf. P. Lond. 267). 2nd century.

1        $\dot{\epsilon}\pi(\iota\beta o\lambda\dot{\eta})$ $(\check{a}\rho o\upsilon\rho a\iota)$ $\beta\, \mathsf{L}\, \bar{\eta}\, \bar{\lambda o}\, \frac{a}{\cdot\cdot\cdot}\cdot$ $(\gamma\iota\nu o\nu\tau a\iota)$

               $[\ldots\ldots$

2        $\sigma\upsilon\nu\pi a..$ $\sigma o(\ )$ $(\check{a}\rho o\upsilon\rho a)$ $\xi o'$ $\kappa a\tau a\lambda(\ )[$

3 $\dot{a}\pi\eta\lambda(\iota\dot{\omega}\tau o\upsilon)\ \dot{\epsilon}\chi\acute{o}(\mu\epsilon\nu a\iota)\ \dot{\epsilon}\gamma\ \beta a\sigma\iota(\lambda\iota\kappa\tilde{\eta}s)\ \Pi\epsilon\tau\epsilon a\rho\psi\epsilon\nu\tilde{\eta}\sigma\iota s\ {}^{'}A\pi\acute{o}\lambda\lambda\omega$-
                        $\nu o s[$

4 $\gamma\iota\nu\acute{o}(\mu\epsilon\nu a\iota)\ \Pi a o\rho\sigma\upsilon\sigma o\acute{\upsilon}\chi o\upsilon\ \tau o\tilde{\upsilon}\ \Sigma a\mu\beta(\tilde{a}\tau o s)\ a\dot{\iota}\gamma\iota a\lambda(\dot{\iota}\tau\iota\delta o s)$
               $\gamma\epsilon\omega\rho\gamma(\epsilon\tilde{\iota})\ {}^{'}E\delta[$

5 $\dot{a}\pi\eta\lambda(\iota\dot{\omega}\tau o\upsilon)\ T\epsilon\kappa\mu\dot{\eta}\iota\tau o s\ \tau o\tilde{\upsilon}\ \Pi\nu\epsilon\phi\epsilon\rho\tilde{\omega}\tau o s\ [a\dot{\iota}]\gamma\iota[a\lambda(\dot{\iota}\tau\iota\delta o s)][$

6 $\tau\tilde{\omega}\ \Pi\epsilon[\ldots\ldots]o\upsilon\ \tau o\tilde{\upsilon}\ {}^{'}A\kappa o\upsilon\sigma\iota\lambda(\dot{a}o\upsilon)\ a\dot{\iota}[\gamma\iota a]\lambda(\dot{\iota}\tau\iota\delta o s)$
              $\gamma\epsilon\omega\rho\gamma(\epsilon\tilde{\iota})\ .\ o\iota s\ {}^{'}I\tau a\lambda o[\ \kappa a\iota$

7 ${}^{''}I\pi\pi\omega\nu o s\ \Psi\epsilon\nu\sigma\nu\epsilon\omega s\ \tau o\tilde{\upsilon}\ \Pi\epsilon\tau\epsilon a\rho\psi\epsilon\nu\dot{\eta}\sigma\epsilon\omega s\ [a\dot{\iota}]\gamma\iota a\lambda(\dot{\iota}\tau\iota\delta o s)$
              $\gamma\epsilon\omega\rho\gamma(\epsilon\tilde{\iota})\ \Pi o\iota s\ \upsilon\dot{\iota}(\grave{o}s)[$

8   καὶ Ἡπολλῶς .φει( )   (γίνονται) ..

9   ἐπ(ιβολὴ) (ἄρουραι) ε η̄ $\frac{\cdot\ \overline{\iota o}}{a\ \text{S}\ \overline{\eta}}$ (γίνονται) ε η̄ λ̄ο

10   παράμμου ἀπηλ(ιώτου) . . . .

     νότου ξο´ ὕρισα καὶ [β]ίβλωι .. δ η̄ ῑο $\overline{\dfrac{\overline{\eta}\ \overline{\lambda o}}{\cdot}}$. [γί-

11   νονται]

12 νότ(ου) ἐχό(μεναι) Ἥρωντος Πέρσεως καὶ Κερ... [.....γε]
     ουχ( ) ἀπὸ Πω[

13   ἐξ (ἀρουρῶν) ε̄ (γίνονται) ῑο ἡ ἐπ(ιβολὴ) Σοκ(νοπαίου
     Νήσου) . . . . καὶ βορρα( ) α[

14   Α..υ.μ.γ( ) Ἰχθυίνδο(υ) τελ( ) Λ..οκρου τοῦ Παορσυσ-
     ούχ(ου) καὶ Ἀκουτ( )[

15   τοῦ Ἡρακλείδου αἰγιαλ(ίτιδος) γεωργ( )

16   ἐπ(ιβολὴ) β d - - -$\overline{\overset{a\ d}{- -}}$- - -   (γίνονται ἄρ.) δ d̄ ῑο

17   παρὰ το(ῦ) βορρα( ) ἐγ μέρους γ η̄ ῑο (γίνονται) α ⌐

18 νότ(ου) ἐχό(μεναι) Πεκμήιτος Πνεφερῶτος ἀ(νὰ) (ἀρτάβας
     πυροῦ) γ (ἄρουραι) α d̄ η̄ ῑο ξ̄ο

19 γινο( ) Παορσυσούχ(ου) τοῦ Σαμβ(ᾶτος) αἰγιαλ(ίτιδος) γεωργ
     ( ) ἐξ υἱ(ῶν) Ἰσ.... βορρᾶ( )

20   πληλ( ) Πετεαρψενῆσις τοῦ Ἀπολ( ) αἰγιαλ(ίτιδος) γεω-
     ργ( ) Τροιση ...μηλ( )

21   ἐπ(ιβολὴ) κη $\overline{\dfrac{\beta\ \text{S}\ \overline{\eta}\ \overline{\iota o}}{\cdot}}$.   (γίνονται) α ⌐ ξ̄ο

22   ἐπι(βολὴ) αλλο( ) σε( ) .... ἐπ(ιβολὴ)......
     καταλ(είπεται) ἡ προκειμένη

173. (Inv. no. AM 11234 A *verso*. 17 × 7 cm.). Tax Register. 2nd century. A list of names with only the patronymics preserved. Four pay 5 dr., eleven pay 6 dr., and three pay 8 dr.

174. (Inv. no. GD 7645 A *verso*. 27 × 8 cm.). Farm account. ca. A. D. 260. Hermopolis. Three columns.

Col. 1

```
]  .ὑπὲρ τι(μῆς) ἄξονος        ϛ σξ
]  .ὑπὲρ τι(μῆς) μηχη..νην    ϛ ρ
]  ..ϛ ιγ´ μηνὸς καὶ
]  καὶ ιβ                      ϛ λϛ
5  ]  ην ποιη...ι               ϛ δ
   ]Παβους                     ϛ κη
```

Col. 2

```
ἄλ(λοι) ἐργ(άται) β´ ἐπισκάπτουσι ...... ἰδίων
ὄνων καὶ ἄλ(λων) ὄνων γ ἐπὶ μισθ-
οῦ λημφέντων τ... ἀπὸ κγ
ἕως κϛ´ ἡμέρ(αις) δ´ ἐργ(άται) η´
5  ὄνοι ιβ´ ὡς τ(οῦ) ā ὄνου ἐκ ϛ β χϝ (γίνονται) ϛ λ δ
[ε]ὶς ἐργ(άτας) ἐκ ϛ δ        ϛ λβ
[ἐρ]γ(άται) β´ ἐπισκάπτ[ουσι .......
......Φαμενώθ ........
```

Col. 3

```
ἐργ(άταις) β´ καθαρίσασι π...ει .....ιχος
τῆς αὐτῆς τῶν βοῶν ὡς τοῦ ā ......ϛ ϛξ
ἄλ(λος) ἐργ(άτης) α´ ἐπὶ ἡμέρ(αις) β´ ......... ὄνων
καὶ μεταφερ( ) αὐτὰ πναϛ.... β´ ὡς τ(ῆς)
5  ἡμέρ(ας)  ϛ δ   / ϛ η
Βησᾶ ἀγροφύλακι .............
ἐργ(άται) γ´ ὑπουργ( )
[ἐρ]γ(άτης) α´ ἐπὶ ἡμέρ(αις) ε´ .....
.... ἰδίων κτηνῶν ..............
```

On the *recto* of this account is P. Princeton 38, which should be dated somewhat earlier than A. D. 250 for these accounts are apparently not much later than the middle of the third century. To he noted is the symbol χϝ in line 5 of the second column used to express 6 obols. This is the interpretation of the curious sign in P. Flor. 322 (Col. 3) where wages are clearly calculated in a tetradrachm of 28 obols. Probably the symbol in P. Lond. V, col. 1 lines 10, 12 should be read as 6 obols instead of 1 chalcous. Similarly in BGU 14 (col. 4) the price of 80 cotylae of oil at 2 dr. 2 ob. is given as 182 dr. 2 ch. This should be 182 dr. 6 ob. and the reading χβ should be χϝ as here.

175. (Inv. no. AM 8941. 8 × 12 cm.). Grain Accounts. 3rd century. This fragment is part of a roll. On the *recto* there are preserved two columns. Col. 1 contains a record of payments of wheat in small amounts varying from 1-10 artabae. The second column has a list of. names of which very few can be deciphered. On the *verso* the payments in wheat are often followed by a sum of money indicating that the wheat was valued at 24 dr. per art. In a few entries a sum in drachmas is given without any record of wheat.

176. (Inv. no. GD 7530. 25.5 × 12.5 cm.). Division of property. 3rd century. Written in a fine clear cursive.

ἀμφοτέρω]ν γυναικῶν μετὰ κυρίου · Ἀρσεῖς μὲν τοῦ ὁμογνησίου
ἀδελφοῦ Τοθῆτος, Σιντοτόης δὲ τοῦ α...[
δευ]τέρας σφραγεῖδος νότου. ἐγ μὲν τοῦ ἀπὸ ἀπηλιωτοῦ μέρους
ἡ πρώτ[η] σφραγίς, ἐγ δὲ τοῦ ἀπὸ λιβὸς τοῦ πρὸς [
]απλῶν, βορρᾶ δημοσία ῥύμη καὶ κατά τι μέρος ἐν τῶι ἀπηλιω-
[τι]κῷ μέρει τῆς προγεγραμμένης αθε[
]ων τῆς Σιντοτόητος πρότερον Δι[ο]δώρου τοῦ καὶ Ἀπολλωνίου
ἐμβάδου πήχων τριακοσίων θ[
5].οηλεις ὡς ἑξῆς δηλοῦται. τόπων μῆκ[ος πρὸ]ς ἀπηλιωτὴν
πήχων δεκαπέν[τε
]ν εἰσόδου καὶ ἐξόδου ἐμβάδου πήχεις δώδε[κα ......] γίνονται ἐπὶ τοῖ[ς] τόποις ω..[
]ν ἐμβάδου πήχων τετρακοσίων ἑξήκοντα τεσ[σάρων · τή]ν τε
πρώτην σφραγεῖδα ε[

1. Cf. Mitt. Chrest. 248 (P Oxy 506). 7 ff.

177. (Inv. no. AM 8944. 12 × 11 cm.). End of a Lease. A. D. 202.

]λ...[......]. δετηνω( )
]..ουμαι[....]μουμειημκαι
[ἐπερ(ωτηθεὶς) ὡμ]ο[λόγησ]ε   Ⳑ ι a   (202/3)

(Hand 2)

Αὐτοκ]ρατόρων Καισάρων Λουκίου Σεπτιμίου Σεουήρου
5 Εὐσεβο]ῦς Περτί(νακος) Ἀραβ(ικοῦ) Ἀδιαβη(νικοῦ) Παρθικοῦ
Μεγίστου

καὶ Μ]άρκου Αὐρηλίου Ἀντωνίνου Εὐσεβοῦς
Σεβασ]τῶν καὶ Πουπλίου Σεπτιμίου Γέτα
Καίσαρος Σ]εβασ[το]ῦ Φαῶφι δ̅.   1 October 202 A. D.

(Hand 3)

Δημητρία ἡ καὶ Ἑρμιόνη
10 δι' αἰμοῦ τοῦ υἱοῦ Ὡρίω(νος). Ἑρμιό(νη)
μεμίσθωκα ὡς πρόκ(ειται).

178.   (Inv. no. GD 7238 C.   3.5 × 7 cm.).   Contract.   A. D. 250/1.

ὁμολογ[ία   Αὐτοκράτορος]
Καίσαρος Γαίου Μεσσίου Κυίντου
Τραιανοῦ Δεκίου Εὐσεβοῦς
Εὐτυχοῦς καὶ Κυίντου Ἑρεννί[ου]
5   Ἐτρούσκου Μ[εσσίου Δεκίου καὶ]
Γαίου Οὐάλε[ντος Ὀστιλιάνου]
Μεσσίου Κυ[ίντου τῶν σεβασμιωτάτων]

179.   (Inv. no. GD 7554.   16 × 19 cm.).   Agreement Concerning Vegetable Garden and Orchard.   5th or 6th century.

ν]ομισμα[........]ὁμολογία[
]ρατας σοῦ ἐπὶ[   ]..[
]ονος ἀπὸ τῶν ὑπαρχό[ντων
τ]ο γιγνόμενον παρ' ἐμοῦ πωμάριον μετ[ὰ
5   ]....[....].. καὶ τ[.....].τοσιδι..ι....ρ[
].αιτούμενον παρ' ἐμοῦ ἐπὶ Παμοῦς [....]φιλο.[
].[..].αι καὶ π[α]ρασχεῖν τῇ ὑμῶ[ν] ειτ...[
]της ἰνδικτίονος καὶ [αὐ]τῆς ἢ κατὰ[.]τούτου......[
]...ίοις ἢ καὶ σὺν θεῷ ὀπώροις παρά...ε[
10   ]Φοιβάμμων ἀπὸ τῆς ἐμῆς κώμης καὶ αὐτὸς .[
ἥμισ]υ μέρος τοῦ γηδίου τοῦ Κλεμετίου Κοτίνου .....[...]
.........[
].πεσναν τοῦ δικαίου τυγχάνοντα τῆς αὐτῆς λ[α]χανίας ..[
]τοὺς περιγιγνομένους ἐξ αὐτῶν καρποὺς ἀντὶ τῆς ε...[
].......ποιῆσαι εἰς τὴν αὐτὴν λαχανίαν ἀμέμπτως φα[

15   ]χόρτω προσομολογῶ δὲ ἐντεῦθεν ἤδη ἐσχηκένα[ι] παρὰ τῆς [
       τ]ῆς ἑκάστης ἑβδομάδος δ...την εξας ἀπὸ παρ[
       ]. παρασχεῖν τὸν φόρον ἐνιαύσιον ἐν τῷ Ἀθὺρ μη[νὶ
             ]τον ..λαβη φιλ.[..]..[
             ]να.....[
20   ]τῆς μισθώ[σ]ε[ως

Traces of two lines on verso. Papyrus broken off on all four sides. Above line 11 five letters, in Coptic style.

180. (Inv. no. GD 7886 C. 14.7 × 11 cm.). Lease of Garden Land. 6th century (?).

      σ]ὺν λάκκω ὁλοκ[λήρω
     λ]άκκου καὶ φυμα..[...].ωσι[
   ? ἁγί]α ἐκκλησία καὶ χρηστηρίοις πᾶσει[
       ].διαδι κώμης Ὅρμου τοῦ Ἑρμοπολίτου[
5 ? ἄρουρα]μία καὶ σχοινοπλόγοις δυσὶ[
        ]ανδίου ἑνὶ καὶ βαστακτὴ φοινίκων[
      ὅ]μοῖα πεντήκοντα καὶ βιβλίον[
    ἀπόστ]ολον καὶ τὸ ἅγιον εὐαγγέλιον[
      ]ζῶα βοικὰ δύο συντιμηθέντα[

181. (Inv. no. GD 7677 A. 9 × 11.5 cm.). Receipt. A. D. 344.

    ὑπα]τείας Φλαου[ίων Λεοντίου
    ἐπ]άρχου τοῦ ἱεροῦ π[ραιτωρίου
    καὶ Σ]αλουστίου κόμιτος [month, day.
    Αὐρ]ήλιος Τιθοῆς Τ[ιθοῆτος
5   ἀπὸ] τῆς Ὀξυρυγχιτῶν [π]όλεως
    ...]..ος τὴν τέχνην δι' ἐμοῦ
    τ]ῆς γυναικὸς [Σο]φίας
    Α]ὐρηλίῳ Κολλ[ούθῳ ...[4-8]...
    ἀ]πὸ τῆς αὐτῆς [πόλεως
10 χαίρειν. ὁμολ[ογῶ ἀπέχειν
    παρὰ σοῦ εἰς λ[όγον τῶν ὑπὸ
    σοῦ χρεωστ[ουμένων
    σί]του ἀρτάβας [[6-10]
    μ]όνας καὶ [[6-10]

15 ..]. καὶ δραχμ[ὰς   ⁴⁻⁸
κυ]ρία ἡ ἀποχ[ὴ   ⁵⁻⁹
κ]αὶ ἐπερωτ[ηθεὶς ὡμο-
λόγησα] ....[

Traces of three or four lines on verso. Completely illegible.

182. (Inv. no. GD 7886 B. 13.7 × 8.0 cm.). Official Report. 3rd or 4th century.

].ρμο[.] ἐνέχητε εἰς τὰ [
]ησιν ..[.]ου πράγματα καὶ καθὼς [
]α φαίνομαι ὑμῖν ὀφείλετε κα[
]το παραφανῆναί μοι μάλιστα [
5]λογος φανῶν ὄντων τῶν κατε[
]αἰσχύνομαι γὰρ ὀχλῆσαι τῷ ἐν[
].το [γ]ὰρ π[..]άτια ἀνήκον ῞τι῾ τῇ διοική[σει
].·[   ]ὑμῶν[

183. (Inv. no. AM 8959 *recto*. 14 × 26 cm.). Official Correspondence. A. D. 345.

['Υπατείας Φλαουίων 'Αμαν]τίου καὶ 'Αλβίνου τῶν λαμπρ(οτάτων)
        τοῦ ἐπ]ιτρόπου Φλαουίου Θεοδώρου
        ].τα ἐκ λοιπάδων κατατρέχοντα
        Φ]λαούιος Φαυστῖνος ἐξάκτορσιν
5   ]ου ἐξαποστῖλαι τὰ ἐκ λοιπάδων
        ]εως τῆς τρίτης παρελθούσης
[ἰνδικτίωνος   ]ος πρὸς τὴν ἐμὴν καθοσίωσιν
        ]β [..]ιων ὃ προύταξεν τῶν
        ]ρίων τῶν πρόσφατον
10   ]πρὸς ὑμᾶς γέγραφα
        ]λοτουτον ἐξαποστῖλαι
        ]ι τῶν ἑαυτῶν ὑπαρχόν-
[των   ]γραμ[ματ]εύσαντες σπουδάσατε
        ]μπερισιν ἀποσταλέντα ἰνδικὰ ἐκ πεμπτ-
15   ἐρ]ρωσθε τὸ καὶ.....
        τῇ]ς δ/ ἰνδικ(τίωνος) καὶ τὰ ἐκ λοιπαζόν-

[των   ]εας ἐπὶ τοσούτω χρόνω δεδραμ( )

           ]χρόνον ἀποστάλκιται εἰς τὴν Ἀλεξανδρέων

[πόλιν   ]φ/ ἐξαπέσταλκε τοὺς καṭανακάσαντας

20   ]εἰς τὴν Ἀλεξανδρέων ἀκολούθως τῷ

           ]αṇολα τὰ εἴδη ἐξαποστῖλαι προσταίτακται

On the *verso* is an account with the heading λόγος ἀργυρίου ἐνεχ..σι ἀπὸ τι(μῆς) σίτου followed by a list of names with payments in artabas usually of a single artaba of wheat and a sum of money in drachmas—one artaba of wheat being equated with 334 talents. Most of the names are illegible.

184. (Inv. no. GD 7635. 21 × 18.6 cm.). Petition. 4th or 5th century. Flavius Asclepiades Hesychius was *praeses* of the Thebaid about 390, but it cannot be certain that this petition was addressed to him.

    Φλαυίῳ Ἀσκληπιάδ[η] ... [

        παρὰ Αὐρηλίου Παμ[..].[....].σṇ.[

    χρεώστας ἔχω ἐξ τὸν αι[

    συνης τὰ πολλὰ ὑπομνησθέν[τ-

5   ὑπερτιθέμενοι περὶ τὴν α[

    τὴν μεγαλοπρέπειαν ὥστε [ἀναγκά-?]

    ζεσθαι ἕκαστον χρεώστην [

    τὸ ὄφλημα ἀποκαταṣ[στ]η[σ-

    τῇ σῇ ἐξọṇσία ạ[

185. (Inv. no. GD 7628. 12 × 22 cm.). Letter Concerning Termination of guardianship. A. D. 162. For surrender of guardianship see P. Bremer 39.

    ....]θεων Θέωνι τῶι

    φιλτ]άτωι   χαίρειν.

    ....]πεις σὺν πᾶσι οἷς ε-

    ....]ας ἐπιτροπεύων μου

5   ἀπ[ὸ] Φαῶφι ἑκκαιδεκάτης   13 October A. D. 160

    τοῦ ἀπεληλυθότος πρώτ[ο]υ   160/161

    ἔτους τῶν κυρίων αὐτοκρατόρων

    Ἀν[τ]ωνείνου καὶ Οὐήρου ἕως

    ἑκκαιδεκάτης Φαμενὼτ τοῦ ἐνεστῶ-   12 March A. D. 162

10 το[ς] δευτέ[ρ]ου ἔτους τῶν αὐτῶν   161/162
κυρίων Σεβαστῶν καὶ συκεε
.....φ....ạ.ῠ.τωι..ψ...ι...
παχι..σεισ..ι.....μερọς
ἐρρῶσθαί σε εὔχομαι
15   εὐτυχοῦντα πανοικεί.
L β′′ Ἀντωνείνου καὶ Οὐήρου
Καισάρων τῶν κυρίων Φα-
μενὼτ ἐκκαιδεκάτης.   12 March A. D. 162

9. φαμενωτ written in above line.

186.   (Inv. no. GD 7642. 5.5 × 16.5 cm.).   Private Letter. A. D. 28.

[ὁ δεῖνα] Ἀρθῶνι τῶι ἀδελφῶι
[χαίρειν] καὶ διὰ παντὸς ὑγιαί-
[νειν.]τι ἐνβέβλημαι
παρὰ Ἀ]μμωνίου (τετράχοα) κε(ράμια) ρα
5 [καὶ παρὰ] Πυρρίου κε(ράμια)(τετρά)χ(οα) ρβ ἐπι
]ε ἀβλάβερον δε-
κα]ὶ Θράσων οὐ δέδω-
[κε πεντ]ακοσίας δεκαὲξ
καὶ Δῖος βουτος
10   ]ψυψις ἐφλβ
]εις οἶνον καλὸν ἀτο-
ἰκ]ανὴν καὶ τὰ πρῶτα
γ]ράψαι περὶ ὧν ἐὰν
[θέλης. ἀσπάζ]ọμạι δὲ Ἀρθώνιον καὶ
15 [τοὺς σοὺς π]άντας. τὰ δ' ἄλλα σαυ-
[τοῦ ἐπιμελο]ῦ ἵν' ὑγιαίνεις.
['Ετους]ιϛ Τιβερίου Καίσαρος
[Σεβαστοῦ] Χοιακ ι′ .
[   ] οὐδὲν χρήσιμον γε-
20 [γένηται]

187. (Inv. no. AM 11235 B. 8 × 19 cm.). Letter. 1st century.

..ν στρωμάτεα τὸ κληθῆν[αι
τοῦ στρώματος ∫ μδ ...[
.μη . αρισι λήμψη ..[
ος καὶ Εὐδαίμωνι καὶ ..[
5 .τῶι φ[ιλ]τάτωι χαίρ[ειν
ντως ἀναγκαῖον γνῶ[ναι?
ἐπιστολῆς ἀσπάσασθαί σε[
ς καὶ τούτους πάντας ἐφ ἧι [
ες ἡμῶν φιλανθρωπία ..[
10 στου τὰ δὲ χρήματα [
μείνας ὡς γράφεις ἐμοὶ [
μόνας ενο............[
ε στατῆρας εὐθέως ἐλάβομεν [

The remainder offers nothing of interest since only a few letters are now decipherable. On the left margin is a reference to something sent by the camel driver Cholus.

188. (Inv. no. AM 11245 B. 8.4 × 13.8 cm.). Letter. This papyrus is broken at top, bottom, and left side. Written in a fine cursive script. 1st or 2nd century. Probably not a reply to P. O. 744 (dated 1 B. C.) although dealing with the same subject.

πρ]ὸ παντὸς ὑγειαίνειν ὡς ἐδήλωσάς μοι
]ων ἔπεμψας ἐπιστολίδιων περὶ τοῦ
]σίου [ἐ]κθεῖναί με. αὐτὸ ἐκτέθεικα
ἐ]ν τῶ Ἀθὺρ μη(νὶ) τὰ σκενάρια δὲ οὐκέ-
5 [τι   ] ἐμοὶ αὐτὰ πωλῆσαι διὰ τὸ ἀγγεῖον εὐ-
]ξαντ[..]ν ἔασα αὐτὰ μέχρι οὗ παρῆνα[ι
ἐ]ὰν βο[υ]λῆ ποιῆσαι. ἐχρησάμην
]λου..ου αρει εἴκοσι διὰ ἀκολάστω(ς)
]δεξαι δὲ αὐτὰς παρὰ Εὐαγγελίου
10   ]...... αὐτῶ γὰρ αὐτὰς δέδωκα
]τελέσας.........ωρα
]ἔπλευσιν σὺν Πομπηείω
]ελησητε. ἐπέμψεσθε
].....ρου ....

15   ]ευρ . . . .
                ]τον σοι αὐτὰς ἔπεμψα
                ] . . . τὸν ἀδελφόν μου
            ἐπε]τήρησα. οἶδε γὰρ κρει. . .
                ]ν αὐτῶ δὲ Πομπηείω
20   ]ἐντέλλομαι ἐκκτός σου ε-
            ἐ]ποίησα θέλουσά σοι πέμψαι φοι-
                ]τους οὐδεὶς ἀνέσχηται ἕως

189. (Inv. no. AM 11230 D. 6 × 13.5 cm.). Letter. 1st or 2nd century.

              Χε[να]νουβ( ) Πε[ν
              τῶ ἀδελφῶ χ[αίρειν
              κόμιζ[ο]ν σπε[υ]δ..[
              ρα παι[δ]ίσκου[
          5   ελαι.. ευπ..πι..[
              οἶδας εἰ μὴ αὐτὸ[
              πέμψον δι' αὐτοῦ η[
              Δῖον ἢ ὃν εὕρης[
              ἔχω μὲν οὐχ εὕρω[
          10 θάνω μετὰ τῆς θυ[γατρὸς
              κατεφρόνη[σ
              τὴν θυγάτρα νεο[γενῆ?   'Α]
              λεξάνδρου καὶ οὐδ[
              σας καὶ διὰ Χαιρήμον[ος
          15 μοι ἄν δὲ γράψας με[θυ-]
              γατέρα μου Χενανουβ[
              τη [ἀσ]πάζεται αὐτὴν[
              αιων σὺν τέκνοις κ[
              αὐτοῦ ἐρρῶσθα[ι εὔχομαι

              Verso

              ἀπόδος Πεν   . . . .
                ἀπὸ Χενα   νουβ.

190. (Inv. no. AM 11245 A. 8 × 18.5 cm.). Private Letter. 2nd century.

Σαρ [. . . . .]δι
τῷ ἀδελφῷ χαίρειν.
π[ρὸ μὲν πάν]των
εὔχομαί σαι ὑγιάνιν
5 κ[α]ὶ τὸ προσκύνημά
[σου] πο[ι]ῶ τῷ κυ-
ρίῳ Σαράπιδι καὶ
[τ]οῖς [πατρῴοι]ς θεοῖς

Several lines follow but in the broken state of the papyrus nothing is intelligible.

191. (Inv. no. GD 7886 B. 18.5 × 12.0 cm.). Letter. 5th century(?). The chief interest in this fragment is the illiteracy of the writer.

ρο
]διλευς τοῦ κ[
]ων καὶ μεσ...ν[
τι
].ια σου ὁπόσα...[
5 μετὰ νβ.. ἐμὲ ἐπὶ δηπάνη ἀδιγούμεθα [
τὰ
καὶ ἔμαθα ὁ ἀδελφὸς Γεώργιος πάντα ἔπαθο[ν
στώματι ἐὰν τενατὼν τίποτε γίνεται ε[
ἀπέρχομε ἐν Κοστανδινοπέλεος σκοπη.[
καὶ γράψον μοι καὶ διὰ τάχους καταλαμένου σοι [

4. δαπάνη?   ἀδικούμεθα
5. ἔμαθε: cf. P Princ. 102.10. τά = ἅ: Mayser I. 69 pp. 310 ff.
6. τενατων = δυνατόν?   γίνηται: Mayser I. 10 pp. 62 ff.
7. ἀπέρχομαι   Κωνσταντινοπόλεως

INDEXES

I. EMPERORS

TIBERIUS

ἔτους δεκάτου [Τ]ιβερίου Καίσαρος Σεβαστοῦ **141**. 6
[ἔτους] ιε Τιβερίου Καίσαρος [Σεβαστοῦ] **186**. 17
(ἔτους) ιθ/ Τιβερίου Καίσαρος **161**. 13
ἔτους δευτέρου καὶ εἰκοστοῦ Τιβ[ερίου Καίσαρος] Σεβαστοῦ **146**. 1
τρίτον καὶ ε[ἰκοστὸν ἔτος] Τιβερίου Καίσαρος Σεβαστοῦ **146**. 14

NERO

β (ἔτος) [Νέρωνος τοῦ] Κυρίου **152**. i. 2
γ (ἔτος) Νέρωνος τοῦ Κυρίου **152**. ii. 4

DOMITIAN

ἕβδομον ἔτος Α̣[ὐ]τ̣οκρά[τορος] Κ̣α̣ί̣[σ]αρος Δομιτιανοῦ Σεβαστοῦ Γερμανικοῦ **147**. 7
(ἔτους) θ Δομιτιανοῦ τοῦ Κυρίου **162**. 15

HADRIAN

ιβ (ἔτους) ['Α]δριανοῦ τοῦ [Κυρί]ου **124**. 17
ιε (ἔτος) 'Αδριανοῦ Καίσαρος τοῦ Κυρίου **124**. 8
ις (ἔτους) 'Α[δριαν]ο̣ῦ [Καί]σαρος τοῦ Κυρίου **124**. 2

ANTONINUS PIUS

(ἔτους) . Αὐτοκράτορος Καίσαρος Τίτου Α[ἰλίου 'Αδριανοῦ 'Αν]τωνίνου Σεβ[αστοῦ Εὐσε]β[οῦς] **121**. 16
(ἔτους) ἐνάτου Αὐτοκράτορος Καίσαρος Τίτου Αἰλίου 'Αδριανοῦ 'Αντωνίνου Σεβασ[το]ῦ Εὐσεβοῦς **125**. 1
κγ (ἔτους) Αἰλίου 'Αντωνίνου **127**. 10

MARCUS AURELIUS

(ἔτους) ιβ' Αὐτοκράτορος Καίσαρος Μάρκου Αὐρηλίου 'Αντωνίνου Σεβαστοῦ 'Αρμενιακοῦ Μηδικοῦ Παρθικοῦ Μεγίστου **148**. 22

MARCUS AURELIUS AND VERUS

πρώτ[ο]υ ἔτους τῶν Κυρίων Αὐτοκρατόρων 'Αν[τ]ωνείνου καὶ Οὐήρου **185**. 6
(ἔτους) β// 'Αντωνείνου καὶ Οὐήρου Καισάρων τῶν Κυρίων **185**. 16
δευτέ[ρ]ου ἔτους τῶν αὐτῶν Κυρίων Σεβαστῶν **185**. 10
γ (ἔτος) 'Αντωνίνου καὶ [Οὐήρο]υ τῶν Κ[υρ]ίων Σεβαστῶν **128**. 8

MARCUS AURELIUS AND COMMODUS

[(ἔτους) –] καὶ δεκάτου Αὐρηλίων 'Αντωνείν[ο]υ καὶ Κομμ[όδου τῶν Κυρίω]ν Σεβαστῶν 'Αρμενικῶν Μηδικῶν Πα[ρ]θικ[ῶν Γερμανικῶν Σαρματικῶ]ν Μεγίστων **149**. 13

COMMODUS

τὴν Αὐρηλίου [Κομ]μόδου 'Αντωνείνου [Καί]σαρος τοῦ Κυρίου [τύχην] **129**. 19

101

Sᴇᴘᴛɪᴍɪᴜs Sᴇᴠᴇʀᴜs

(ἔτους) δ Αὐτοκράτορος Καίσαρος Λουκίου Σεπτιμίου Σεουήρου Εὐσεβοῦς
Περτίνακος Σε[β]αστοῦ Ἀραβικοῦ Ἀδιαβηνικοῦ **131**. 15

Sᴇᴘᴛɪᴍɪᴜs Sᴇᴠᴇʀᴜs ᴀɴᴅ Cᴀʀᴀᴄᴀʟʟᴀ

Αὐτοκρατόρων Καισάρων Λουκίου Σεπτιμ[ίου] Σεουήρου Εὐσεβοῦς Περτίνακ[ος
Ἀ]ραβικοῦ Ἀδι[αβηνικοῦ] Παρθικοῦ Μεγίστου καὶ Μάρκ[ου] Αὐρηλίου
Ἀντ[ωνίνου] Εὐσεβοῦς Σεβαστῶν **130**. 14

Sᴇᴘᴛɪᴍɪᴜs Sᴇᴠᴇʀᴜs, Cᴀʀᴀᴄᴀʟʟᴀ ᴀɴᴅ Gᴇᴛᴀ

[Αὐτοκ]ρατόρων Καισάρων Λουκίου Σεπτιμίου Σεουήρου [Εὐσεβο]ῦς Περ-
τί(νακος) Ἀραβ(ικοῦ) Ἀδιαβη(νικοῦ) Παρθικοῦ Μεγίστου [καὶ
Μ]άρκου Αὐρηλίου Ἀντωνίνου Εὐσεβοῦς [Σεβασ]τῶν καὶ Πουπλίου
Σεπτιμίου Γέτα [Καίσαρος Σ]εβασ[το]ῦ **177**. 4

Eᴀʀʟʏ Tʜɪʀᴅ Cᴇɴᴛᴜʀʏ

[ἔτους τρ]ίτου [Αὐ]τοκρ[άτορος Καίσαρος ―――― Εὐσεβοῦς Ε]ὐτυχο[ῦς Σε-
βαστοῦ] **144**. 1

Dᴇᴄɪᴜs, Dᴇᴄɪᴜs ᴀɴᴅ Hᴏsᴛɪʟɪᴀɴᴜs

[Αὐτοκράτορος] Καίσαρος Γαίου Μεσσίου Κυίντου Τραιανοῦ Δεκίου Εὐσεβοῦς
Εὐτυχοῦς καὶ Κυίντου Ἑρεννί[ου] Ἐτρούσκου Μ[εσσίου Δεκίου καὶ]
Γαίου Οὐάλε[ντος Ὁστιλιάνου] Μεσσίου Κυ[ίντου τῶν σεβασμιωτάτων]
178

Dɪᴏᴄʟᴇᴛɪᴀɴ

ὁ ἐν θεοῖς Διοκλητιανός **119**. 9

Dɪᴏᴄʟᴇᴛɪᴀɴ ᴀɴᴅ Mᴀxɪᴍɪᴀɴ

ἔτους [ἐννεακ]αιδεκ[ά]του καὶ (ἔτους) ιη/ [τῶν δεσποτῶν] ἡμῶ[ν] Διοκλητιανοῦ κα[ὶ Μαξιμιανοῦ Σεβα]στ[ῶν καὶ (ἔτους) ια Κωνσταντίου καὶ
Μαξιμιανοῦ τῶν ἐπιφανεστάτων Καισάρων] **133**. 14

Aɴᴀsᴛᴀsɪᴜs

πάντα νικῶ[ντος] θεοῦ καὶ δεσπότου ἡμῶν [――――] Φλ(αουίου) Ἀναστασίου
τοῦ αἰωνίου Αὐγούστου α[ὐτοκράτορος] **139**. r. 7

II. CONSULS AND INDICTIONS

a. Consuls

[ὑπα]τείας Φλαου[ίων Λεοντίου ἐπ]άρχου τοῦ ἱεροῦ π[ραιτωρίου καὶ Σ]αλουσ-
τίου κόμιτος **181**. 1

[ὑπατείας Φλαουίων Ἀμαν]τίου καὶ Ἀλβίνου τῶν λαμπρ(οτάτων) **183**. 1

τοῖς τὸ δ μετὰ τὴν ὑπατίαν Φλαουίου Βασιλίου τοῦ λαμπρ(οτάτου) **154**. 1

b. Indictions

2nd　**158**. 2
3rd　**183**. 6
4th　**183**. 16
10th　**134**. i. 2; **154**. 2

III. MONTHS

IV. PERSONAL NAMES

Γ..μολ 140. p. 1. v. ii. 1
Γαῖος 163. 1, 12; son of Zoilus, 135. 15
Γεβοσε 140. p. 2. v. i. 9
Γεώργιος 191. 5; Αὐρήλιος Γ., ἀρχισταβλίτης, 145. 11

Δανιήλ 140. p. 2. v. ii. 23
Δανιήλιος 140. p. 2. r. i. 8, ii. 12, v. i. 17
Δαρ.α 140. p. 2. r. i. 3
Δεῖος 149. 1, 2
Δημητρία 177. 9; daughter of Sarapodorus, 131. 5
Δημήτριος, see Τινήιος
Δημοκράτης, father of Diodorus 131. 9
Δημοσθένης = Heroninus, father of Nicomedes, 126. 7
ἄπα Δι( ) Σαι( ) 140. p. 1. v. ii. 2
Δίδυμος = 'Απολλώνιος, 131. 6
Αὐρήλιος Διογένης 144. 3, 22, 24
Διόδωρος 176. 4; father of Ischyrion, 124. 19; son of Democrates, 131. 9
Διονυσία 123. ii. 1
Διονύσιος 119. 1, 8; 141. 3, 9; 149. 2
Διόσκορος 119. 2, 6, 22; Δ. Σωσικλῆς 131. 7; Δ. = 'Ισχυρίων 126. 3; Δ., father of Areion, 134. iii. 1; Δ., father of Atiana, 134. iii. 5; Δ., father of Philoxenus, 149. 2; Αὐρήλιος Δ. 151. 4
Δῖος 161. 1; 186. 9; 189. 8; δημόσιος γραφεύς, 148. 27; ἄπα Δῖος Σαι( ), 140. p. 1. v. ii. 2, p. 2. r. i. 17
Διόφαντος 126. 1
Δουλίας 140. p. 2. r. i. 1

Εἰδῶς 166. 1, r.
Εἰρήνιος, father of Panus, 135. v. 16
Εἰσάριον 151. 8
Εἰσοπολιτ( ) 140. p. 1. v. i. 10
Ἔλαος 140. p. 1. r. i. 6
Ἐλιουζγ 140. p. 1. v. i. 16, 19
Ἔλλος 129. 12
Ἐνκιτο( ) 140. p. 2. r. ii. 6
Ἐπιφ 140. p. 1. v. ii. 16
Ἐπιφαλίμιος 140. p. 2. v. i. 12
Ἐπιφάνιος Δαρ.α 140. p. 2. r. i. 3
Ἔππιος, father of Pouoris, 152. ii. 1

Αὐρήλιος Ἐριεύς 167. 1
Ἑρμᾶς 123. ii. 23; father of Horus, 132. 2, 4
Ἑρμίας 129. 3
Ἑρμιόνη 177. 9, 10
Ἐσοῦρις 123. iii. 7; son of Horion, 134. ii. 8
Εὐαγγέλιος 188. 9
Εὐδαίμων 187. 4
Ευθ( ) 132. 14
Ευθο[132. 32
Εὐλόγιος 137. 4, 6; 138. 7; father of Anouphis, 135. v. 2
Εὐσέβιος 138. 1
Εὐσωφύριος, son of Pekos, 130. 2; father of Orsenouphis, 130. 7
Εὐφημία, daughter of Anoup, 145. 12

Ζαλλ( ) 140. p. 2. v. ii. 24
Ζαχαρία 140. p. 1. v. i. 14, ii. 17
Ζώειλος 168. 3
Ζώιλος 116. 7; 127. 1, 13; father of Gaius, 135. v. 15
Ζώσιμος 125. 3

Η[....]θ 140. p. 2. v. ii. 5
Η[....]ν 128. 2
Ἡλίας Μαρίας 136. r. 5
Ἡπόλλως 172. 8
Ηρα[132. 9
Ἡραΐς 154. 4
Αὐρήλιος Ἡρακλειανός = Μωρίων 133. 2
Ἡρακλείδης, son of Symmachus, 137. 1; father of Akout( ), 172. 15
Ἡρακλη( ) 132. 13
Ἡράκλῃος 123. ii. 11, iii. 13
Ἡρακλῆς 123. ii. 18, 19; Ἡ. Μετάβολος 135. 17
Ἡρᾶς 126. 1; = Αὐνᾶς, 147. 4
Ἡρώδης, father of Hierakiaena, 147. 1
Ἥρωις, father of Athenarion, 125. 4
Ἥρων, son of Mystharion, 128. 2(?), 4; father of Horion, 134. 13
Ἥρων (gen. Ἥρωντος) 172. 12
Ἡρωνῖνος = Δημοσθένης 126. 6

Θαῆσις ἡ Χ... 117. 2
Θακῶρις 123. i. 16
Θαμῖνις 160. 1

Κολλαῦθις 142. 9, 13
Κολλαῦθος 123. ii. 14, 15
Κολλοθ( ) Ταπιο( ) 140. p. 2. v. i. 4
Κολλοῦθος, Κ. Ταπι., 140. p. 1. r. i.
    12; Αὐρήλιος Κ., 181. 8
Κόπιος 135. v. 3
Κόσμος 126. 3
Κότινος, Κλεμέτιος Κ., 179. 11
Κοφοκ 140. p. 1. v. ii. 20
Κουφο( ) 140. p. 1. r. ii. 2
ἄπα Κυρι 140. p. 1. v. ii. 14
Κυριακός 140. p. 1. r. i. 6, v. ii. 15
Κωνσταντῖνος 140. p. 2. r. i. 12
Κωνστάντιος 135. v. 14

Λαλ...[ ] 123. iii. 1
Λάος Νωός 140. p. 2. r. i. 14
Λε...... 140. p. 1. r. i. 1
Λεκα( ) Ταματι( ) 140. p. 2. v. i. 5
Λεόντιος Λ. Πορτ( ) 140. p. 2. r. ii. 8;
    Λ. .ρ 140. p. 2. v. ii. 18
Λεπτὸς Κιλ( ) 140. p. 1. v. i. 12
Λεωμαι Εἰσοπολιτ( ) 140. p. 1. v. i.
    10
Λιτ( ) 140. p. 2. r. i. 16; ἄπα Λιτ( )
    140. p. 1 r. i. 9
Λο( ) 140. p. 1. r. i. 14
Λογγινία 150. ii. 2
Λυκαρίων, father of Aurelius Ly-
    carion, 151. 1; Αὐρήλιος Λ., son of
    Lycarion 151. 2

Μακάριος Κόπιος μικρός 135. v. 3
Μακρόβιος, son of Dioscorus, 119. 2
Μάλιος 152. 1
Μαρεψῆμις 146. 4, 5, 7, 9, 18
Μαρίας, Ἡλίας Μαρίας, 136. r. 5
Μάρκος 131. 4; Μ. Πετρώνιος 150. ii.
    9, 10
Μαρσισοῦχος 146. 7, 13, 16, 18
Μάρων 124. 4
Μέλλων 148. 2
Μέμιος 150. i. 2
Μένος, father of Horus, 132. 1
Μεσουῆρις 123. iii. 4
Μετάβολος 135. v. 17
Μῆνος, son of Charesius, 140. p. 1.
    r. i. 5; Μ. Ἀάνιρε 140. p. 2. v. i. 8;
    Μ. Κανα( ) 140. p. 1. v. i. 20;

Μ. Κλαμησία 140. p. 1. v. i. 17;
    Μ. Παάμ 140. p. 1. v. i. 6
Μηνύθευς 139. v. ii. 10
Μοσαιο( ) Παοφιλ( ) 140. p. 2. v. ii.
    13; cf. 140. p. 2. r. ii. 4
Μύλων, father of Harmiusis, 147. 5
Μυσαῖος 140. p. 2. r. ii. 4; cf. 140.
    p. 2. v. ii. 13
Μυσθαρίων 128. 4
Μυσθᾶς 123. iii. 2
Μωρίων = Ἡρακλειανός 133. 2

Αὐρήλιος Νε[ ] 118. 30
Νειλάμμων, father of Pasis 134. i. 6
Νεῖλος 131. 1; 142. 3, 13; 157. 4;
    father of Timaeus, 135. v. 4;
    father of Papontos, 135. v. 18
Νεκθερῶς 130. 18; 148. 6
Νεκφεραῦς 123. iii. 3
Νεκφερῶς 123. ii. 10, 22, 24
Νεμείων, son of Titanus, 152. ii. 6
Νεπωτιανός = Ἀπολλώνιος 131. 3
Νέστωρ 168. 1
Νεχθώτης, father of Hatres, 130. 1;
    father of Petestheus, 130. 5;
    father of Nechthotes, 130. 6; son
    of Nechthotes, 130. 6; son of
    Pseuderetes, 130. 8
Νήδυμος 130. 19
Νιγέρεα 150. ii. 2
Νικίας 157. 7
Νικόδημος, father of Heroninus, 126.
    7
Νοκνε 140. p. 1. v. i. 24
Νον.. 140. p. 1. r. i. 13
Νουνε 140. p. 1. r. i. 8
Νοως 140. p. 1. v. ii. 11

Ξένων 123. iii. 7

Οἰνο[130. 18
Ὀλύμπιος 123. iii. 10
Ὄλυμπος 144. 5, 7
Ὀνήσιμος 123. iii. 6
Ὀνθον[130. 20
Ὀννῶφρις 123. ii. 4
Ορ[ ], father of Constantius, 135.
    v. 14
Ὀρσενοῦφις, son of Eusophyrius, 130.
    7

Πλουτίων, son of Belanus, **135**. *v.* 22

Πμῶχ[ις] **132**. 1, 5

Πνεφερῶς **152**. i. 8, 14, ii. 17; **160**. 3; father of Tekmeitus, **172**. 5, 18

Πόις **172**. 7

Πολλῶς **123**. ii. 20

Πομπηεῖος **188**. 12, 19

Πορτ( ) **140**. p. 2. *r.* ii. 8

Που( ) **140**. p. 2. *v.* ii. 19

Πουῶρις, son of Eppius, **152**. ii. 1

Αὐρήλιος Πρασῦτις, son of Victor, **154**. 5

Προσοπ( ) **140**. p. 1. *v.* ii. 10

Πτολεμαῖος **117**. 13; **123**. iii. 27; **150**. ii. 1

Πτολλαῦς **123**. ii. 5

Αὐρήλιος Πτολμίων **133**. 1

Πύρριος **186**. 5

Πωη( ) **140**. p. 1. *v.* i. 14

Σαι( ) **140**. p. 1. *v.* ii. 2, 4, 6, p. 2. *v.* i. 18

Σακαῶν, son of Satabous, **134**. i. 7; son of Pemoutius, **134**. iii. 7

Σαμ( ) **140**. p. 2. *r.* ii. 5

Σαμβαθίων **123**. ii. 25

Σαμβᾶς **123**. ii. 23; father of Paorsy-souchus, **172**. 4, 19

Σαμβοῦς **123**. i. 12, 14, 24, 27, ii. 10

Σάμψων Ἰσάκ **140**. p. 1. *v.* ii. 5; Σ. Κάρπα **140**. p. 2. *r.* i. 11; Σ. Καρτ( ) **140**. p. 2. *v.* i. 20; Σ. ... **140**. p. 2. *r.* i. 19

Σάννω Σι( ) **140**. p. 2. *v.* ii. 17

Σαρ[ ] **190**. 1

Σαραπάμμων **131**. 1; son of K., **135**. *v.* 21; brother of Chaeremon, **164**. 1

Σαραπίων **117**. 15, 19, 23; **119**. 15; **120**. 11; **128**. 7; son of Penech-therotus, **130**. 4

Σαραπόδωρος, father of Demetria, **131**. 5

Σασνᾶ **140**. p. 2. *v.* ii. 9

Σασνῶ **140**. p. 1. *r.* ii. 12, p. 2. *r.* ii. 7

Σάσων υἱός **140**. p. 2. *r.* ii. 7

Σαταβοῦς, father of Sakaon, **134**. i. 7; father of Allion, **134**. ii. 6

[Σεμπ?]ρονία Σεουηρείνου **118**. 18

Σεν( ) Σκατ( ) **140**. p. 1. *v.* i. 23

Σεπάκυρος Ἀνατολι( ) **140**. p. 2. *r.* i. 5

Σεράνος **150**. ii. 4

Σερᾶς, father of Aeias, **134**. ii. 4

Αὐρήλιος Σερῆνος **144**. 5, 6, 21

Σι( ) **140**. p. 2. *v.* ii. 17

Σι.ε.νο...... **140**. p. 2. *r.* ii. 13

Σίγνος **140**. p. 2. *v.* ii. 20

Σῖμος **140**. p. 1. *v.* i. 18

Αὐρηλία Σιντοτόη = Ἀλειτάριον **133**. 6

Σιντοτόης (gen. Σιντοτόητος) **176**. 1, 4

Σισόις **123**. iii. 15, 23, 24, 25, 26

Σίτανος **140**. p. 2. *r.* ii. 10

Σκατ **140**. p. 1. *r.* i. 7, *v.* i. 22, 23

Σκοῖπος, father of Apollos, **152**. ii. 11

Σουαι( ) Ταναιε **140**. p. 2. *r.* i. 9

Σοφία **159**. 12; **181**. 7

Συ( ) Σαι **140**. p. 2. *v.* i. 18

Σύμμαχος, father of Heracleides, **137**. 1

Συρι( ) **140**. p. 1. *r.* i. 10

Συριακός **135**. *v.* 8

Σωσικλῆς = Διόσκορος **131**. 7

Τ..μθις **123**. i. 1

Αὐρήλιος Τ.ρυ...ν **167**. 2

Τααρμῶτις **123**. ii. 22

Ταβιθᾶ **140**. p. 1. *v.* ii. 13

Ταβούριος **152**. ii. 16

Ταγῶς **123**. ii. 28

Ταγῶτας **123**. i. 29

Ταγῶτις **123**. ii. 4

Ταλο( ) **140**. p. 1. *r.* ii. 5

Ταματι( ) **140**. p. 2. *v.* i. 5

Ταμύσθα **123**. i. 2

Ταναιε **140**. p. 2. *r.* i. 9

Τανεκφερῶς **123**. i. 19

Τανεμγεύς **123**. ii. 18

Τάνεμις **123**. i. 20

Τανετβῆς **123**. i. 8, 9

Τανομγεύς **123**. ii. 27

Τανοῦβις **123**. ii. 2

Ταορσενοῦφις **123**. i. 21

Ταπετσῖρις **123**. ii. 20

Ταπεύς **123**. ii. 11

Ταπιο( ) **140**. p. 1. *r.* i. 12, p. 2. *v.* i. 4

Ταποντῶς **129**. 17

V. OFFICIAL AND MILITARY TERMS

VI. TRADES AND PROFESSIONS

VII. HONORIFIC TITLES

ἀδελφότης 120. 2
ἀρετή 137. 1; 169. 4
δεσπότης 137. 1; 170. 1
ἐνδοξότατος 139. r. 9
εὐσέβεια 119. 24
εὐσεβής, τὰ ε. τελέσματα, 119. 51
εὔτονος, τῆς σῆς ε. ἐπεξελεύσεως, 118. 3

θαυμασιότης 145. 3
κύριος 120. 11
λαμπρότατος 129. 6; 137. 1, 4; 183.
  1; see also II and VIII.
μεγαλοπρέπεια 184. 6
μισοπονηρία, ἡ σὴ μ. 119. 4
περίβλεπτος 137. 2

VIII. GEOGRAPHICAL INDEX

A. *Peoples, Nomes, Districts*

Ἀρσινοίτης νομός 144. 3, 10; 146. 3
ἐπαρχία 119. 50
Ἑρμοπολίτης νομός 137. 2; 180. 4
Ἑρμωνθίτης νομός 118. 31, 32
Ἡρακλείδου μερίς 123. iii. 20
μερίς, Ἡρακλείδου μ. 123. iii. 20;
  Πολέμωνος μ. 124. 11
μέση τοπαρχία 141. 7
μητροπολίτης 124. 9
νομός 126. 4; 127. 5; Ἀρσινοίτης ν.,
  144. 3, 10; 146. 3; Ἑρμοπολίτης ν.,

137. 2; 180. 4; Ἑρμωνθίτης ν., 118.
  31, 32; Ὀξυρυγχίτης ν., 131. 2
Ὀξυρυγχίτης νομός 131. 2
Πέρσης τῆς ἐπιγονῆς, see index XII,
  s. v. ἐπιγονή
Πολέμωνος μερίς 124. 11; 146. 3
Πουατβ, τόπος Π. λεγόμενος, 149. 5
προάστιον, χωρίον π., 158. 4
τοπαρχία, μέση τ., 141. 7
τόπος, τ. Πουατβ λεγόμενος, 149. 5
χωρίον προάστιον 158. 4

B. *Cities, towns, and villages*

Ἀλεξάνδρεια 127. 4; 162. 3; 183. 18,
  20
Ἀρσινοειτῶν [πόλις] 149. 1
Βακχιάς 149. 5
Βούβαστις 129. 9
Ἑπτὰ κῶμαι 132. 27
Ἐνεργετίδων πόλις 126. 2
Ἡφαιστιάς 150. i. 18, ii. 8
Θεαδέλφεια 121. 2, 12; 125. 5; 127. 7;
  128. 2; 134. i. 2.
Θωνι[ ] 130. 19
Ἰβίων 151. 4
Ἴσιδος πόλις 132. 25
Κ[ ] 120. 11
Κοινοτηθερατ[ ] 132. 29
Κοστανδινοπέλεος = Κωνσταντινοπόλεως
  191. 7
Λυκόπολις 148. 29

μητρόπολις τοῦ Ἑρμωνθίτου νομοῦ 118.
  32
Νέσλα 147. 10, 24
Νηδυμ( ) 130. 19
Νῆσος Μεσοποταμία 148. 7
Νίκιον 148. 2
Νκαλαχει 132. 18
Ὀξυρυγχιτῶν πόλις 154. 5; 181. 5; ἡ
  λαμπρὰ καὶ λαμπροτάτη Ὀξυρυγχειτῶν
  πόλις, 133. 3
Ὀξυρύγχων πόλις 147. 2
Ὅρμος 180. 4
Πανι( ) 138. 2
Πέλα 131. 8, 11
Πτεροφόρου ἐποίκιον 124. 15
Πτολεμαΐς Εὐέργετις 144. 2
Πω[ ] 172. 12
Σένις 148. 8, 11

IX. RELIGION, SUPERSTITION, AND MAGIC

X. TAXES AND FEES

ἀπογραφή:
κατ᾿ ἄνδρα ἀ., **127**. 9
κατ᾿ οἰκίαν ἀ., **127**. 11 ; **129**. 8
διαπεῖσμα **138**. 6
εἶδος **125**. 4, 8 ; **126**. 2, 5 ; **146**. 20 ;
183. 21
εἰσφορά **119**. 47
ἐκφόριον **137**. 3, 5
ἐπαρούριον **125**. 9
ἐπιβολή **172**. 1, 9, 13, 16, 21, 22
εὐθενία στρατιωτική **119**. 21
καταλοχισμῶν τέλη **131**. 2
κόλλυβος **125**. 9
κωμητικά **124**. 15
λαογραφία **124**. 1

ναύβιον **125**. 5, 9
ναῦλον **168**. 2, 3
ὀκτάδραχμον σπονδῆς Διονύσου **125**. 6,
10
προσδιαγραφόμενον **125**. 5, 7, 9, 10
προσμετρούμενον **138**. 6
σπονδή **131**. 14 ; σ. Διονύσου, **125**. 6
σὺν κ **136** *passim*
σὺν ρ **136** *passim*
τέλεσμα **119**. 51 ; **146**. 19
τέλη **131**. 8 ; τ. καταλοχισμῶν, **131**.
introd.
τελωνικά **132**. 6
φόρος **132**. 34

XI. MEASURES, WEIGHTS, COINS

ἀργύριον **125**. 6 ; ἀργυρίου δραχμαί, **141**.
2 ; **144**. 8 ; **149**. 7 ; **150**. i. 15 ; **152**.
ii. 11 ; **156**. 3
ἄρουρα (Ⱡ) **126**. 8 ; **131**. 9 ; **134**.
passim ; **135**. *r*. 2-4 ; **136** *passim* ;
146. 8, 11 ; **147**. 11, 13 ; **148**. 8, 9,
11, 12 ; **149**. 6 ; **150**. i. *passim*, ii.
6, 7 ; **172** *passim* ; **180**. 5 (?)
ἀρτάβη (⚊) **117**. 7, 29 ; **136** *passim* ;
138. 5 ; **147**. 15 ; **151**. 12 ; **172**. 18 ;
181. 13
denarius (✳) **143**. 2
δέσμη **136** *passim*
δίχοον (χ^β) **153**. 6
δραχμή (ſ) **125**. 7, 10 ; **130**. *passim* ;
131. 13, 14 ; **133**. 12, 13 ; **141**. 2 ;
142. 5 ; **144**. 8, 25 ; **148**. 12 ; **149**.
7 ; **150**. i. 16, ii. 12 ; **152** *passim* ;
155 *passim* ; **156**. 3 ; **174** *passim* ;
181. 15 ; **187**. 2
κεράμιον : κ. τετράχοον, **186**. 4, 5
κεράτιον (/) **140** *passim* ; π ═ παρὰ

κεράτια **139**. *v*. i. *passim*
λίτρα (λι) **139**. *r*. 3
μέτρον ἁδρόν **147**. 26
μέτρον Σεράπιδος **147**. 28
μέτρον τετρασχυνεικόν **147**. 26
μνᾶ **142**. 7 ; **167**. 11
νόμισμα (νο) **136**. *r*. 1, 4, *v*. 9 ; **139**.
v. i. *passim*, ii. 7 ; **140**. p. 1. *r*. i. 14,
ii. 12 ; **140**. p. 1. *v*. i. 12, ii. 8, 10,
12, 16, 17 ; **145**. 14 ; **179**. 1
νομισμάτιον **154**. 9
πῆχυς **176**. 4-7
πο( ) **135**. *r*. *passim*
στατήρ **187**. 13
σχοινόπλογος **180**. 5
τετράχοον (χ^δ) **153**. 6, 8 ; **186**. 4, 5
τετρωβέλιον (F) **174**. ii. 5
τριωβέλιον (Γ) **152**. i. 12, ii. 3
χαλκός **125**. 5
χοῖνιξ **136**. *r*. 6 ; **136**. *v*. 7, 8, 10
χοῦς **163**. 3

XII. GENERAL INDEX

ἀποκαθίστημι **184**. 8
ἀποστέλλω **119**. 48; **183**. 14. 18
ἀπόστολος, see index IX.
ἀπύτακτος **148**. 10
ἀποτάττω **161**. 10
ἀποτίνω **147**. 29
ἀπόφασις **118**. 6, 14
ἀποχή **181**. 16
ἀπόχρεια **141**. 8
ἀραβών **145**. 6
ἀργέω **119**. 58
ἀργύριον **141**. 2; **142**. 5; **183** *v.*; see
　also index XI.
ἀρετή, see index VII.
ἀρίθμησις **125**. 8; **133**. 8
ἀριστερός **142**. 2
ἀρτάβη, see index XI.
ἄρτι **159**. 17
ἀρτίως **119**. 23
ἀρτοκόπος, see index VI.
ἀρτυματοπωλής, see index VI.
ἀρχή **116**. 6; **119**. 25
ἀρχισταβλίτης, see index V.
ἀσπάζομαι **166**. 3; **186**. 14; **187**. 7;
　189. 17
ἄσπορος γῆ **134** *passim*
ἀσφαλίζω **166**. 5
ἀτελής **119**. 27
αὐλή **129**. 10
αὔριον **162**. 9; **165**. 3
αὐτή, used of a woman acting for
　herself without a guardian, **131**. 4
αὐτόθι **149**. 9
ἀφηλικότης **119**. 16
ἀφίστημι **120**. 4
ἄχρι(ς) **119**. 14; **130**. 13; **144**. 17

βαρύς **120**. 3
βασιλικὴ γῆ **134** *passim*; **172**. 3
βαστακτή **180**. 6
βεβαιόω **146**. 18; **147**. 20; **149**. 9
βεβαίωσις **146**. 19; **149**. 10
βενεφικιάριος, see index V.
βιβλείδιον **118**. 4, 9, 21; β. Ἰούλιον,
　118. 29
βιβλιοθήκη Ἀπολλιναρίου **144**. 20
βιβλίον **127**. 3; **180**. 7
βίβλος **172**. 11
βοηθός, see index V.

βοϊκός **180**. 9
βορρᾶς **172**. 13, 17, 19; **176**. 3
βούλομαι **117**. 10, 22; **144**. 18; **148**.
　3; **151**. 5; **162**. 3; **188**. 7
βοῦς **174**. iii. 2
βουτος **186**. 9

γαμετή **145**. 12
γείτων **149**. 7
γένημα **138**. 3
γένος **124**. 13; **148**. 5
γεομετρία **147**. 13
γεωργέω **117**. 14; **119**. 12, 26, 38;
　136. *r.* 5; **146**. 9; **172** *passim*
γεωργός **128**. 3; **168**. *v.* 11; see also
　index VI.
γῆ **119**. 7, 12, 43; **147**. 17; **150**. i. 10,
　13, 23, ii. 7
γήδιον **119**. 26; **179**. 11
γιγνώσκω **119**. 23; **187**. 6
γλυθύ **155**. *r.* 10
γναφεύς, see index VI.
γονή **151**. 16
γόνυ **142**. 2
γράμμα **120**. 2; **139**. *r.* 4 (?); **141**. 5;
　145. 16
γραμματεῖον **145**. 9, 14
γραμματεύς, see index V.
γραφεῖον **141**. 7
γραφεύς, see index VI.
γράφω **117**. 12, 15; **118**. 10; **137**. 1;
　141. 4; **145**. 10, 15; **148**. 27; **149**.
　12; **150**. i. 5; **160**. 2; **161**. 3, 4, 11;
　162. 6, 8; **163**. 2, 7; **183**. 10; **186**.
　13; **187**. 11; **189**. 15; **191**. 8
γυνή **120**. 5; **160** *v.*; **168**. 1; **176**. 1;
　181. 7

δανείζω **144**. 25
δαπάνη **152**. i. 1, ii. 3
δαψιλής **165**. 8
δεδραμ( ) **183**. 17
δεξιός **146**. 8
δέομαι **119**. 38
δεσπότης **119**. 55; **120**. 10; **169**. 1, *v.*;
　170. 1; ὁ δ. Θεός, **120**. 9, see also
　index I and VII.
δεύτερος **118**. 21
δέχομαι **120**. 2; **145**. 5

XIII. LATIN WORDS

GPSR Authorized Representative: Easy Access System Europe - Mustamäe tee
50, 10621 Tallinn, Estonia, gpsr.requests@easproject.com